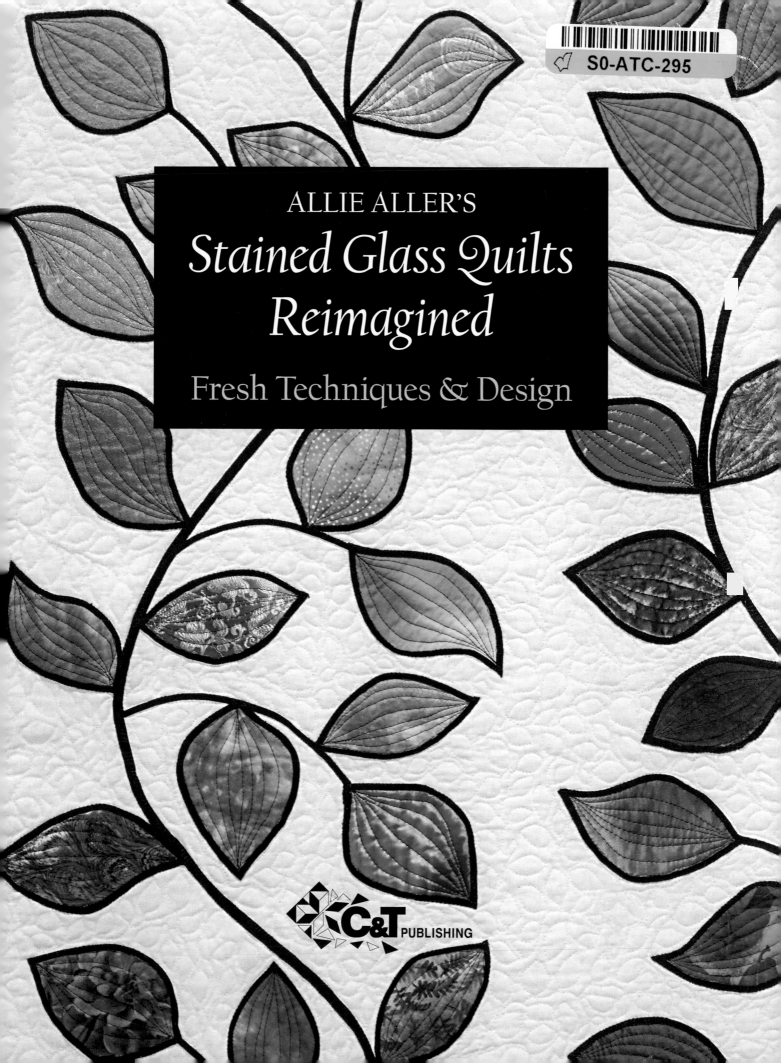

# ALLIE ALLER'S
# *Stained Glass Quilts Reimagined*

## Fresh Techniques & Design

C&T PUBLISHING

Text copyright © 2017 by Allie Aller

Photography and artwork copyright © 2017 by C&T Publishing, Inc.

Publisher: Amy Marson

Creative Director: Gailen Runge

Editors: Liz Aneloski and Donna di Natale

Technical Editors: Susan Nelsen and Amanda Siegfried

Cover/Book Designer: April Mostek

Production Coordinators: Tim Manibusan and Joe Edge

Production Editor: Alice Mace Nakanishi

Illustrator: Valyrie Gillum

Photo Assistant: Carly Jean Marin

Photography by Diane Pedersen of C&T Publishing, unless otherwise noted

Published by C&T Publishing, Inc., P.O. Box 1456, Lafayette, CA 94549

Library of Congress Cataloging-in-Publication Data

Names: Aller, Allie, 1954- author.

Title: Allie Aller's stained glass quilts reimagined : fresh techniques & design.

Other titles: Stained glass quilts reimagined

Description: Lafayette, CA : C&T Publishing, Inc., [2017]

Identifiers: LCCN 2016026419 | ISBN 9781617452864 (soft cover)

Subjects: LCSH: Quilting--Patterns. | Patchwork--Patterns. | Glass painting and staining--Patterns.

Classification: LCC TT835 .A45725 2017 | DDC 746.46--dc23

LC record available at https://lccn.loc.gov/2016026419

Printed in China

10 9 8 7 6 5 4 3 2 1

# Dedication

*For my boyfriend, best friend, and husband, Robert,*
*who truly is the man of my dreams.*

*Man of My Dreams*, 16″ × 18″, 2015

# Acknowledgments

There are three great artists whose work has inspired my love affair with stained glass quilts: Louis Comfort Tiffany, Maxfield Parrish, and Frank Lloyd Wright. Their sense of color and design has fed my soul for decades and first prompted my foray into this quiltmaking genre 25 years ago.

I have many people in the here and now to thank as well, starting with Tess Hall Neri, Dale Kastle, Mary Corbet, Holly Casey, and Patty Young for their contributions to this book. Thanks go to Georgia Granato of the incomparable Fabric Depot in Portland, Oregon, and to my friend Lisa Plooster Boni, for being my sounding boards. Those listed in the Favorite Supplies section generously contributed their quality products to the making of my quilts, and I sincerely thank them. I feel great gratitude to Gailen Runge, the creative director of C&T Publishing, for letting me run with this project; to Liz Aneloski, my editor, for helping me mold it into shape; and to Susan Nelsen, my technical editor, who surefootedly led me out of some sticky thickets.

Here at home, all love to my husband, Robert, for his unwavering support and his valuable input … not to mention his homemade pizza with that killer homegrown sauce.

# Contents

# PROJECTS

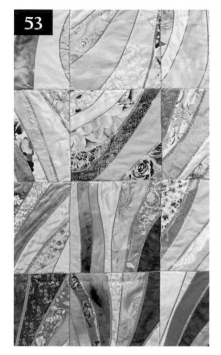

**53**

*Windy Sunshine*
a summer throw

**60**

*Leaf Vine*
a bed quilt

**68**

*Mondrian's Window*
a couch quilt

**78**

*Window for Frank*
an improvisational couch quilt

**83**

*Welcome Wreath*
a wool and cotton wallhanging

**88**

*Tiffany's Peacock*
a classic stained glass wallhanging

All quilts made by Allie Aller

# Introduction

Back in the 1990s, I spent several years developing my own techniques for making stained glass quilts—and I made a lot of them. Then crazy quilting burst into my life, and sixteen joyous years of hand stitching flew by. But recently, in the mysterious ways of the muse, I was drawn back again to my earlier stained glass work, wanting to discover more.

*The Attendant*, 60″ × 66″, 1997
Photo by Bill Bachhuber

When I think about it, there were three main reasons for my change in direction. The first was the graphic nature of stained glass quilts. Composition, color, line, shape, and fabric choice are all paramount; texture is secondary, embellishment just about nonexistent. This was a refreshing change and challenge to me as a designer. My attraction to stripped-down design was also no doubt influenced by the Modern Quilt movement going on all around me.

Another reason for renewing my work in stained glass quilting is how quickly these quilts come together. While some are intricate and require patience, once you are familiar with the processes in this book you will see that these quilts can be completed relatively quickly. We get to work with lots of new fabrics and projects this way!

Finally, the challenge of pushing the envelope in this quilt genre to make it new again was irresistible. I have poured everything I have learned and loved into this book in the hopes that you can explore your own ideas and take your own stained glass quilts further, too. There is no bias tape to be found on these pages, and you can adapt the approaches presented here to any style of quilting that you love.

Chapter One examines how to source, develop, and work with your own designs. Which supplies and construction methods to use with these new approaches to stained glass quilting are covered in Chapter Two. Chapter Three has the nitty-gritty step-by-step information on the three main techniques I've used throughout the book—couching, appliquéd ribbon and trim, and iron-on leading—as well as some introductory exercises. The gallery showcases these techniques "in action," and the six projects will help you to practice them yourself. Three full-sized pullout patterns enable you to dive right in. Two of them are simple; the other will keep you busy for a while. Four of the projects are functional quilts and two are decorative, with many variations presented.

So, welcome! I'm delighted that you are here.

*—Allie*

# 1 Design Sources and Strategies

The stained glass quilts presented in this book are both functional quilts and decorative wallhangings. While the functional quilts use block patterns or overall piecing layouts, the wallhangings generally require a pattern design. But where do you look for inspiration and how do you make your *own* pattern? This is the focus of this chapter.

Many areas of design can lend themselves to stained glass quilt work. Indeed, if you think of stained glass quilting as "outlined" art, any design based on simple line drawings or shapes can be transformed into a pattern.

First we will look at the plethora of design resources available to us today. Next we will talk about options for enlarging your design of choice to the size quilt you wish to make. After that, I share different methods for transferring those designs to fabric. Finally, I will give you a start-to-finish example of creating a little quilt from a homemade pattern to illustrate these ideas.

## Pattern Ideas Are Everywhere

When I first explored stained glass quilting many years ago, I quickly discovered that appliqué patterns lend themselves to the outline technique used for stained glass quilts. And what a wealth of design inspiration there is in the appliqué world, to be sure!

Page through your collection of appliqué books and see what intrigues you as a possible stained glass design. With the techniques we will cover in this book you will be able to create a pattern from what you like and then make it. (Of course, all copyright laws apply; you may create patterns for your personal use from publications and designers' work, but you may not profit from them. This does not apply to vintage designs that are out of copyright.)

*Stained Glass Poppies*, 32½″ × 32½″

An interpretation of the cover quilt of Nancy Pearson's *Floral Appliqué: Original Designs and Techniques for Medallion Quilts* (EZ Quilting by Wright's, 2000)

# Needlework and Vintage Designs

Blackwork is a needlework technique that requires charted geometric line drawings. These designs can be easily adapted for our use. If you do an Internet image search on the term *blackwork*, you will be amazed at what comes up. This is a great source of inspiration and design.

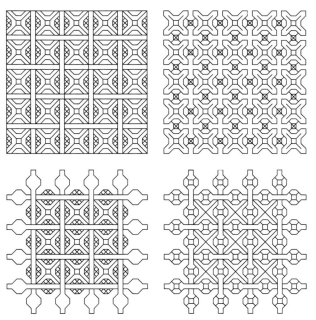

Blackwork designs by Mary Corbet

Do you love those old embroidery transfers from the 1930s? What whimsical stained glass projects could grow from those! These designs can be found on eBay and at local estate sales, or they may already be waiting for you in a drawer at home.

How about redwork? Again, the line-drawing aspect of redwork transfers quite well to stained glass quilt design. (See the practice quilt, *Turkey in the Corn*, page 11.)

If you are looking for shapes to arrange into your own pattern, as I was for *Modern Rose Window* (page 44), a great source is disassembled silk or fabric flowers, pressed flat. You can find all shapes of flowers at craft stores. You can also use flowers made with any die-cutting system you have.

These custom fabric flowers are from M&S Schmalberg (see A Few of My Favorite Supplies, page 98). I used freezer-paper templates made from these in *Modern Rose Window* (page 44).

One more source worth noting is the free Antique Pattern Library online (antiquepatternlibrary.org). This site provides an unending supply of scanned antique design books from every field of creative craft endeavor from decades and even centuries past.

*Henri's Window* is based on a design from *Dessins de Vitrerie* by Henri Carot (1886). New Media Arts, Inc., which runs the nonprofit Antique Pattern Library, kindly gave me fair use permission to use this printed screenshot from the website.

Printout from the Antique Pattern Library website

*Henri's Window*, 22½″ × 26¾″, 2015

Keep in mind that the designs you find can be simplified if necessary—you don't want an extreme amount of detail, but you can achieve quite a bit of complexity using the techniques in this book.

## Coloring Books and Clip Art

What could be more directly translatable into a stained glass pattern than a coloring book image? There are so many to choose from, on any and all subjects, in book form or as downloadable images from the Internet.

Dover Publications has put out stained glass coloring books for years, and the designs in them are ready-made for us. Dover's series of clip art books is a wonderful source of copyright-free imagery, too.

C&T Publishing (ctpub.com) also has a series of coloring books with many designs adaptable to quilt work.

Design from *Playful Designs Coloring Book* by Patty Young (available from C&T Publishing)

*Silk Rose Window*, 22″ × 22″

Look at the little quilt called *The End* (page 97). The design was inspired by a motif in *Paisleys and Other Textile Designs from India* by K. Prakash (Dover Publications, 1994). The leading was laid out on a wholecloth background with the glass colors painted in afterward using thickened craft ink, just like a coloring-book page.

## Internet Searches

Pinterest has myriad imagery on stained glass, stained glass quilts, stained glass patterns … any way you type in your search, great inspiration will appear like magic on your computer screen.

Or you can do image searches for stained glass windows that you love, just to soak them up and be inspired. Cathedral rose windows and Louis Comfort Tiffany's landscape windows are my personal favorites, and I know my love for them comes out in my work. *The Attendant* (page 6) is based on Tiffany's work, as is *Tiffany's Peacock* (page 88). What do you love best? Go find it and be inspired.

## Purchased Patterns

You can simply go to a stained glass supply store or website and find patterns, in any style you like, to use for your quilts. Nothing could be easier than that.

# Tutorial: How to Develop Your Own Pattern

The original redwork Turkey block

*Turkey in the Corn*, 16½″ × 19½″, 2015 (See full-size pattern, pullout page P1.)

Let's go through the process of converting a vintage redwork Turkey block into a pattern the size we want, and using it to create this small stained glass wall quilt of a proud tom turkey.

Refer to these steps any time you are creating your own pattern.

1. Create a line drawing from a photograph or scan (see Create a Line Drawing from a Photograph, page 12). Print it.

2. Trace the design onto tracing paper. If necessary, simplify the design (see Simplify the Line Drawing, page 12).

3. Create and use individual glass pattern templates (see Create and Use Your Individual Glass Pattern Templates, page 15).

4. Transfer the pattern design to the background fabric (see Transfer the Pattern Design to the Background Fabric, page 16).

5. Working from back to front, lay out the glass fabric shapes on the background fabric (see Place the Pieces on the Background, page 16).

Now let's look at each of these steps in more detail.

# Create a Line Drawing from a Photograph

I use a freeware program called IrfanView to work with my photo, and I will use it in my example. But you should use the photo program you are familiar with.

I open my photo and go through the following process:

1. From the Image menu, I select Convert to Gray Scale. This converts my photo to black and white.

2. Again under Image, I choose Effects. The submenu has Edge Detection. I click on that. The image will look black with faint white lines.

3. Then I click Negative, and the image is reversed in value so that the edge detection shows up as dark lines.

4. I like to finish by clicking the Sharpen button on the Image menu.

5. Save this photo; I named it "Turkey Edge Detection."

6. My image will now be in black and white with the shapes outlined, but it will still be too "busy" for a stained glass quilt.

The next step is to print this image and trace it onto tracing paper, simplifying the design.

---

# Simplify the Line Drawing

1. I tape my printed edge detection photo to a flat surface, overlaying it with some quality tracing paper.

2. I may need to make a few tracing "overlays" to get my drawing exactly the way I want it. I'll just keep taping tracing paper over my last drawing, refining little things each time, removing extraneous lines or tweaking the shapes a little bit. Tracing paper and pencil lead are cheap; it is worth spending some extra time on this step.

I went through 4 "finished drawings" before my turkey drawing was finally to my liking!

3. When the drawing is finished and I know the shapes are suitable for the stained glass technique I'll be using, the next step is to resize it to the pattern size I want.

That brings us to the next subject: How to resize a pattern.

The printed edge detection photo (*left*) and the small, traced, and refined finished drawing (*right*)

# Resize the Finished Drawing to the Desired Size

Consider the following options for any line drawing you've chosen from the sources discussed earlier, whether from a coloring book page, a photograph you've worked with, or some other source.

## Copy Shops and Blueprinters

You can take your finished drawing to a copy shop (such as Kinko's) that has a wide-format printer, and have a copy made to the exact size you specify. To continue with our turkey example, I wanted my drawing to be 13″ × 13″ square. So I set the machine according to its instructions, and out came my pattern.

You can also take your drawing to a blueprint shop, especially if your project will be very large. (I once made one that was 12′ × 17′—yes, that's *feet*. The blueprinter had to print it in sections, but I got the full-size pattern I needed by taping it together at intervals of 12″. It really was massive.)

In case you do not have access to storefront services like these, following are three other options.

## Enlarge the Drawing Yourself

### USE A CRAFT PROJECTOR

Inexpensive projectors designed especially for crafters shine an image placed under them onto a wall. You fix a piece of paper to the wall and trace over the projected image, with the size of the projected image determined by the projector's distance from the wall.

There are two drawbacks to this method. The first is that you need a completely darkened room (or closet) to get the clarity you need for tracing. The second is that it is sometimes hard to get the exact size you want to project onto the wall; it takes a lot of fiddling while in the dark. But for small projects like our turkey, this method is fine.

### USE THE GRID METHOD

Anyone can use this tried and true technique.

1. Begin by lightly drawing a grid over your drawing (or on a piece of tracing paper that you place over your drawing).

2. On paper the desired size of your finished pattern, draw a comparable grid, scaled to the size you want. So if your small drawing is divided into 36 squares, with 6 lines horizontally and vertically, your large paper should have a grid of 36 squares as well.

3. Square by square, copy and draw the shape within each square in the small grid onto its corresponding square in the large grid. Use a pencil with a good eraser, and keep a sharpener nearby.

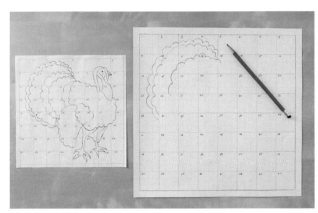

Small gridded drawing and the larger-grid copy

4. When the large grid is filled in completely, lay a large sheet of tracing paper over it and trace the completed drawing. Now you have it to size with no grid marks.

The drawbacks to this method are that it takes a lot of time and the accuracy might suffer a bit.

There are many great resizing programs out there. The one I like is an inexpensive and easy-to-use one called Rapid Resizer (rapidresizer.com). I use it all the time because it is fast and effective, and I don't have to drive anywhere or pay anyone to get my pattern enlarged to exactly the size I want.

I simply upload a photograph of the finished drawing based on my edge detection photo, and I type in the size I want the finished pattern to be. If the drawing fits on your scanner, scanning is an even better option. Save the scan as a JPG and upload that to the program.

The program creates a PDF of my drawing that is printable on separate 8½″ × 11″ sheets. It is very simple to assemble the printed pages into a whole image with tape.

I then trace over the assembled pattern pages onto a large piece of tracing paper to get the finished drawing, and then I am ready to create the pattern pieces.

> **Tip**
>
> *You can also resize the edge detection photo as is, loading it into Rapid Resizer. After you tape together the pages to create the whole image, you can make all the necessary tracing-paper overlays from this resized printed image to refine the final drawing. This allows you to work at a larger scale as you finalize the pattern. I developed Tiffany's Peacock (page 88) this very way.*

The finished drawing enlarged with Rapid Resizer (*left*) and the full-scale traced drawing (*right*) with glass fabric shapes numbered in the order in which they will be laid out. See the pattern (pullout page P1).

## Create and Use Individual Glass Pattern Templates

I looked at several photographs of tom turkeys online in order to get a good sense of what colors to use for the glass fabrics. You can do that too with your image, or try coloring on a tracing-paper copy of the finished drawing to determine the look you want.

Keep these important points in mind as you create templates:

• In my approach to stained glass quilting, you generally do not need to fold under the edges of the glass fabrics before you place the leading over them. The fabrics are laid out with raw edges on a foundation or background fabric, and the leading hides those raw edges. But you do need a seam allowance for the edges of the pieces that are overlapped. You don't want the raw edges simply butting up against each other.

• So when you create the individual pattern pieces from the finished, resized drawing, draw in seam allowances, but only on those edges that are overlapped by neighboring shapes.

• The overlapping is in turn determined by the sequence in which the shapes are laid down on the foundation. It is always best to start at the back and move to the front, as in any appliqué project. In the turkey example, the shapes in the drawing are numbered accordingly.

• Draw all the templates on a master template drawing. Trace over each individual template with a second piece of paper to use when you are ready to cut out fabric. You may wish to refine a shape or two; the master template drawing is very handy for making these slight changes along the way.

The master template drawing, showing the finished edges with a solid line and the extra ¼″ seam allowances with a dotted line. Nearby is my pile of small scraps, ready for cutting out into shapes.

### Transfer the Pattern Design to the Background Fabric

There are many methods for doing this. The one you choose will depend on the characteristics of the background fabric. Lightweight, lighter-colored fabrics and opaque, dark ones require different approaches.

- Use a lightbox to trace the design onto lightweight, lighter-colored fabric, such as quilter's cotton or silk. If you don't have a lightbox, tape the drawing to a window and then tape the fabric over it for tracing.

- If you are using a very lightweight foundation fabric such as muslin and covering the entire foundation with glass fabrics, simply tape the pattern to your work surface with the muslin taped over it. You will be able to see the pattern through the fabric and can position your glass pieces accurately that way. There is no need at all to trace the pattern onto the fabric, thus saving a step. This is exactly how *Henri's Window* (page 9) was laid out, as well as all the leading lines in *The End* (page 97).

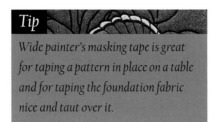

**Tip**

*Wide painter's masking tape is great for taping a pattern in place on a table and for taping the foundation fabric nice and taut over it.*

- For dark fabrics, the pounce method works well. Make a copy of the final drawing of your pattern. Using a large needle in your sewing machine, but no thread, sew over all the lines of the pattern. Then tape the background fabric to a table and the perforated pattern over it. Lightly use a chalk pounce over the taped pattern to fill the holes with chalk. Carefully lift off the perforated pattern, and your design is in place. *Silk Rose Window* (page 10) was marked this way.

---

- As another method for dark fabrics, such as the denim used in our turkey, you can trace the outline of the final drawing onto freezer paper, cut it out, and iron it onto the background fabric. Outline it carefully and then pull off the freezer paper. As you begin to lay out the glass shapes, you will know you are retaining the accurate overall shape of the design.

Cut-out freezer-paper shape of the whole turkey (*left*); cut fabric turkey shapes being placed on the marked foundation (*right*)

### Place the Pieces on the Background

I use spray adhesive for large pieces and pins or glue dots for smaller ones to keep them in place until I am ready to add the leading.

# How to Work with No Pattern at All

Let's be honest: some of us just don't enjoy patterns and would rather work without one. Spontaneous collage—defined here as an artistic composition of fabrics pasted over a surface, often with unifying lines and color—lends itself very well to stained glass quilt work.

Improvisational piecing can be the basis for a stained glass quilt, and even the leading can be spontaneous. *Turkey in the Corn* (full quilt, page 11) has some improvisational leading work to place its whimsical subject into context: a cornfield, of course! I drew lines spontaneously on the background fabric and then applied leading over them. When the leading lines were sewn down, they performed dual duty, providing quilting lines over the entire surface of the piece.

Now that we have the tools to create our own designs, let's dive deeply into some new technical approaches to this beloved genre of stained glass quilting. We will examine fabric choices, supplies, tools, and leading techniques in Chapter Two (page 18). In Chapter Three (page 29), we'll use these techniques in some exercises to prepare for the projects.

There is a lot to cover, but don't worry, there is no bias tape involved!

# 2 Glass and Leading— Supplies and Approaches

Starting in the 1980s, almost all stained glass quilts were made with bias tape as the leading. While these quilts were lovely, I personally thought they took too long to make, and their static look made me want to push the envelope visually.

In this chapter, we will go over the new concepts that I've worked with in stained glass quilting, and the supplies and tools needed to create with them. The next chapter will use these approaches in exercises to familiarize you with the techniques involved. Let's have a look. …

## Glass Fabrics

I've learned that many kinds of fabric, not just cotton, are welcome for use as glass in stained glass quilts.

### Silks and Silk Blends

The reflective nature of the silk fiber translates beautifully into stained glass quilting. *Mondrian's Window* (page 68) uses both silk and 50/50 silk/cotton blends. The luminosity of the fabrics and saturation of the colors give a much more vivid impact than 100% cotton could. Quilting them increases the angles of light reflected off their surfaces. Plaid silks are also used to great—and deceptive—effect in *Mondrian's Window.*

Hand-dyed silks are a precious treasure. They are expensive, so I end up using them as small but oh-so-delicious additions to my compositions. Again, you can see what a rich element they add to the solids in *Mondrian's Window.*

*Silk Rose Window* (page 10) showcases silk brocades. Not only do the fabrics have a subtle sheen, but the motifs fussy-cut from the woven brocade patterns add a pleasing (and in this example symmetrical) complexity to the glass shapes.

Detail of *Silk Rose Window* (page 10)

An array of silk fabrics: cotton/silk blends, plaids, hand-dyed silks, and brocades

## Batiks

Every quilter loves batiks, and we all have them in our stash. Their saturated colors and tonal qualities are wonderful in stained glass quilts. I used them extensively in *The Parrish Farm* (page 43). I think they work best in a group, creating a mood all their own.

## Cotton Solids

In quilting, this is the golden age of the solid, with many fabric companies having lines of 300 colors or more. While cotton solids do not have the sheen of silk, again, when grouped, they give a modern and clean feel to a contemporary stained glass quilt project. Also, they come in charm packs, which offer an easy way to get a lot of colors in the small amounts needed for these quilts.

Charm packs, such as this one from Michael Miller Fabrics' Cotton Couture line, were used to make *Henri's Window* (page 9) and *Modern Rose Window* (page 44).

## Wool

Why not? Wool, too, attains lovely color saturation when dyed and imparts an unexpected twist in stained glass quilting. Plus, it is very easy and nice to work with. See *Love Wreath* (page 47) and *Welcome Wreath* (page 83).

## Other Fabrics In and Out of the Mix

In *Leaf Vine* (page 60), I combined all the previously listed fabrics and some oddball ones too, such as velveteen, polyester, and even flannel. Mixing things up can be a lot of fun and a serendipitous way to dig into your stash (especially if you do any crazy quilting, as I do, and have lots of fancy fabric scraps).

I used a wide range of fabrics as the glass leaf shapes in *Leaf Vine* (page 60). In this mix are cotton (velveteen, print, batik, seersucker, brocade, flannel), hand-dyed fabrics, silk (velvet, taffeta, dupioni, brocade, and kimono fabrics), and metallic polyester.

A word about prints … I personally don't use busy prints with lots of contrast in stained glass quilting, as I think they can distract from the graphic nature of the genre. That said, author Angela Besley uses heavily patterned prints to wonderful effect in her book *Rose Windows for Quilters* (Guild of Master Craftsman Publications, 2000). The bottom line: Just go with what you love.

Fabrics to avoid: Any overly heavy fabric with a lot of texture or nap is problematic because it does not work well with the leading. Fabrics that fray easily can give you headaches. Also, I don't advise using meltable fabrics, such as some polyesters or acetates. You don't want to accidentally iron any holes into your quilt top.

Above all, you need to be able to keep things flat. You may be adding quilted texture later, but in stained glass quilting, a flat top adds to the believability, you might say, of the piece.

# The Three Stained Glass Approaches

What is essential to actual stained glass—and by extension, stained glass quilting-—is that the shapes within the composition are outlined. In real stained glass, this is of course functional; the leading holds the pieces of glass in place. For those of us working in fabric, however, the leading is primarily a visual component, though it does serve the purpose of covering the raw edges of the glass fabric shapes. Also, for quilters, those outlines don't always have to be black.

Here are the three approaches I use to apply the leading, with a few visual examples to introduce you to them.

## Couched Leading

Couching is laying down a thick fiber on the surface of the quilt and sewing it into place with a second thread—in our case, a fine thread. Couching is a great approach for in-the-ditch leading on and between quilt blocks, but it can be used to surround appliquéd shapes as well. We can vary the thickness of these leading lines by using thicker or thinner couched fiber.

*Couched Vintage Blocks*, 23″ × 23″, 2015

I think stained glass–style couching works particularly well in bringing some snap to vintage blocks. See also *Stained Glass Wheels* (page 49).

## Appliquéd Leading

Appliqué, in this case, means adding ribbon or trim by machine. The finished edges of ribbon and trim, and their variety of widths, make them excellent for leading. They are great along long, straight seams, but you can bend and appliqué them along slight curves as well. Again, these work well in an in-the-ditch situation.

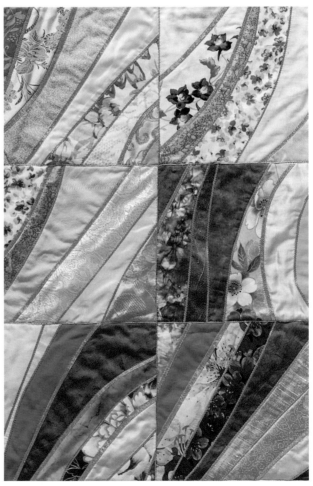

Detail of *Windy Sunshine* (page 53). Three different widths of metallic trim are appliquéd between the glued glass patches (see The Glue Appliqué Method, page 55). Note the heavy gold metallic thread couched between the blocks.

# Iron-On Leading

Fusing is by far the most versatile approach and is terrific for raw-edge collage designs on a background fabric.

The leading fabric is prepared by ironing fusible web to the back. What this means is that any fabric that can take a hot iron can be used for leading, as long as it is handled gently and does not have too loose a weave. My fabric of choice is solid black quilter's cotton, available everywhere.

Next, the prepared fabric is cut on the bias into very fine strips using a ruler and rotary cutter. These narrow lines of leading are fused into place between the glass shapes that are laid out on the quilt top, outlining them and covering their overlapped raw edges.

The last step is sewing these leading strips down with a zigzag stitch using clear thread.

This technique has three very important capabilities:

- It lets us easily cut varying widths of leading strips, from ¹⁄₂₄″ to ½″ wide or more. Being able to incorporate thick and thin lines adds dynamism to a stained glass quilt's design. Landscape quilts in particular benefit from the perspective gained from thin lines in the background and thicker lines in the foreground. (See *The Parrish Farm*, page 43.)

- Because the strips are cut on the bias, they can be ironed around curved shapes very easily. Very delicate shapes can be outlined, and you can achieve very fine detail with the thinnest strips, including very sharp points.

Piles of leading in three different widths, ready for fusing. I think of them as pasta, in this case angel hair, linguine, and fettuccine.

Detail of *Fern Vine* (page 67). The small, detailed shapes and narrow leading dictated that machine zigzagging and quilting be accomplished in the same step.

- If the completely laid-out quilt top—the glass all laid out with its leading fused into place—is then layered over batting and backing, the process of sewing down this ironed-on leading can function as quilting in the same step. There are times when this feature is very appropriate and important.

As you look through this book, you will see that within these three approaches are many variations. Let's look at the various supplies we can use to achieve so many different looks.

Detail of *Modern Rose Window* (page 44). Green leading? Why not! Note that some of the green cotton leading fabric has been cut into small whole leaves to augment the design.

# Leading Supplies and Tools

## So Many Leading Choices!

These leading choices fulfill three essential functions: The first is that their finished or stabilized edges give a clean line; the second is that we can achieve different widths with them; the third is that they are all applied by machine, either couched or appliquéd.

All the leading supplies used in this book are represented in the examples here. They are all shown actual size, so you can get a really good look at them. Next to each leading example is a description of what it is and how it is applied (see Chapter Three, page 29, for specific techniques).

### Finished-Edge Leading

**A.** Acrylic yarn with a tight twist. Glue basted and machine couched. To get a clean line, a tightly twisted, non-fuzzy acrylic yarn is best, one that doesn't get smooshed out of shape by the sewing machine as it is being sewn down.

**B.** Perle cotton #3 thread. Glue basted and machine couched.

**C.** Metallic braid #8 and ⅛″ ribbon. Glue basted and machine couched. DMC perle cotton #3, Kreinik braid #16, and ⅛″ metallic ribbon are also good choices for these fine lines.

**D.** Metallic trim in ⅛″, ³⁄₁₆″, and ¼″ widths. Glue basted and machine appliquéd. Metallic trims of different widths can be purchased by the yard in the bridal department of any sewing store. They are inexpensive.

**E.** Rickrack in ⅛″ and ½″ widths. Glue basted and machine appliquéd. Rickrack can be purchased everywhere, but the ⅛″ width is less common. Find it on Amazon or other craft supply sites online. Rickrack also comes in ¼″, ⅝″, and wider widths.

**F.** Rayon velvet ribbon in ⅛″, ¼″, ⅜″, ⅝″, ¾″, and ⅞″ widths. Glue basted and machine appliquéd. If your local quilt shop doesn't have rayon velvet ribbon, find it online at eBay, Amazon, CheepTrims, M&J Trimming, or other craft supply sites. For a project like *Mondrian's Window* (page 68), I buy complete 25-yard spools.

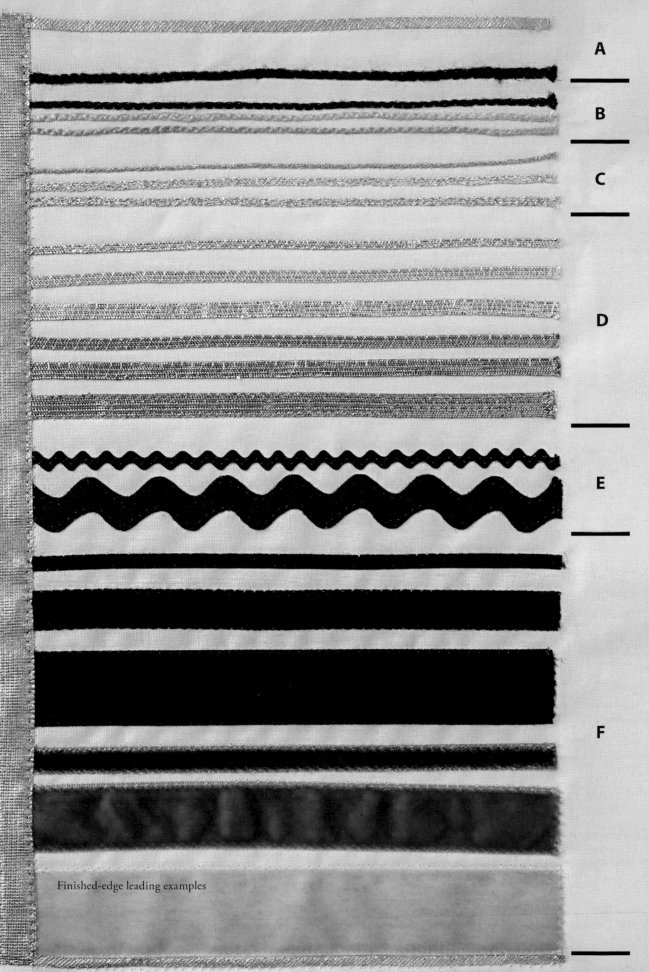

A

B

C

D

E

F

Finished-edge leading examples

## Fabrics for Iron-On Leading

Here is more helpful information based on my two decades of experience working with these techniques and supplies.

• Ironing fusible web to the back of a fabric will stabilize it and prepare it for being sliced into thin bias strips of leading. The fusible then allows the leading to be ironed into place, even in very intricate situations. A lightweight fusible is best, so that the strips can stay flexible when being ironed around a curve. Mistyfuse and Soft Fuse are my brands of choice (after much experimenting).

• Fabrics need to have a fine enough weave that they can hold up to being sliced very thin, and they mustn't fray easily. They need to be able to withstand an iron hot enough to melt the fusible web, so obviously some fabrics won't work. A simple black cotton solid is my favorite choice for all the fusible black leading used in this book. You can find it everywhere, but once you open your mind to the idea of different-colored leading (see *Modern Rose Window*, page 44), the design possibilities are endless.

• Some hard-to-find fabrics are terrific for creating metallic leading that looks like it has been covered in gold leaf. Bonded lamé is fabulous; if you can find it, buy it! Stretch silk knit in gold is also great because it doesn't ravel as most silk will, and it has a subtle and beautiful sheen.

Fused-fabric leading examples: Iron-on bias-cut fabric strips in cotton, silk/Lycra knit, and bonded lamé. Fused and machine appliquéd.

• Another deluxe choice is Ultrasuede, because it can be sliced very thin, has deeply saturated color, and doesn't fray. But at $70/yard and up, it should be saved for a very special project.

Leading supplies

# Tools

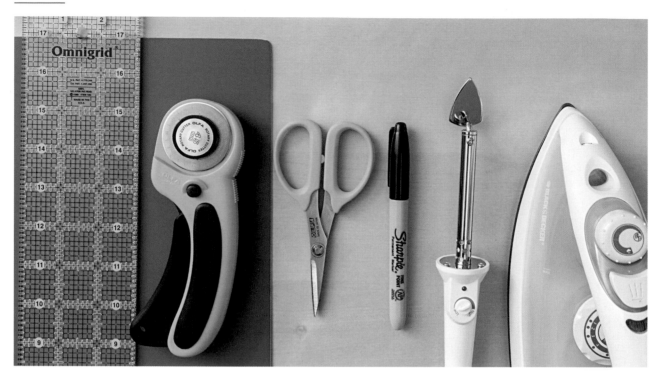

These are essential:

• Small, very sharp scissors

• A new blade in your rotary cutter and even a new ruler and cutting mat. When you are slicing up piles of fine leading, you want a perfect cut and a straight line every time. Old rulers can get nicked up and warped. Mats can get gouged up or start to buckle. Buy yourself some new tools and you will be so glad you did.

• The right iron. The Clover Wedge is very good for delicate work, as is the Clover Mini Iron. I've also found that a small $10 Proctor Silex iron sold at my local discount store works well. Why? Because it is very small and lightweight, heats up quickly, and

stays on. It's not the best for ironing large pieces of fabric, but for ironing down leading, you can't beat it.

• A fine-tip black permanent marker. If bobbin threads pop up, making dots in your black leading, or if you find a gap in your ironed-on leading here or there, a quick touch of the fine tip of the marker takes care of it. Think of it as fine-tuning for your leading. All the quilts in this book have benefited from this trick!

In the next chapter we will learn and practice these techniques, and we will start cutting, gluing, ironing, and sewing. So are you ready?

*Let's Go*, 5½″ × 25½″, 2015

# 3 Glass and Leading Techniques— with Practice Exercises

We've learned some new leading concepts, gone over fabrics and supplies, discussed the best tools, and seen some examples of these new approaches to stained glass quilts.

Do please try these exercises before beginning any of the projects that follow, and then reread these guidelines. I want you to be prepared to have great success from the beginning and really enjoy yourself as you work.

Before we dive into the actual leading techniques, there is one more subject to discuss: which method of quilt construction works best with each technique.

## Quilt Construction Options and Leading Techniques— What Works Best Together

• **Couched fiber** works best for pieced blocks. The seams within and between the blocks are a perfect grid for in-the-ditch leading. A block's character can be completely transformed when each patch is outlined; when a vintage block is couch-leaded, it can gain a contemporary, graphic look. (See *Couched Vintage Blocks*, page 21, and *Stained Glass Wheels*, page 49.)

Detail of *Couched Vintage Blocks* (page 21)

Detail of *Stained Glass Wheels* (page 49)

• **Appliquéd velvet ribbon or trim** works best along seams, or as lines within a whole piece of fabric. Gentle curves are possible as well as straight lines. The impact is bold! (See *Mondrian's Window*, page 68, and *Window for Frank*, page 78.)

Detail of *Mondrian's Window*

Detail of *Window for Frank*

• **Fused iron-on leading** is terrific for fine detail. Glass fabrics with raw edges can be laid out on a fabric foundation, with the leading then covering all the edges. Because this kind of leading can be cut very thin, with practice you can surround very tiny fabric shapes. (See *Fern Vine*, page 67.)

Detail of *Fern Vine*

You can also use this technique to outline images within a whole piece of printed fabric. (See *Vintage Wholecloth Stained Glass*, page 45, and the border of *Henri's Window*, page 9.)

Detail of *Vintage Wholecloth Stained Glass*

Detail of *Henri's Window*

When fused leading is treated as the line element of a composition, the lines not only add to the look of the piece but act as quilting lines in a functional sense as well. (See *Turkey in the Corn*, page 11.)

And finally, you can use this technique to create a coloring book–style design, coloring in the shapes after the leading has been ironed into place on a background fabric. (See *The End*, page 97.)

Detail of *Turkey in the Corn*

Detail of *The End*

**With these principles in mind, let's get started. ...**

# Couched Leading

Technically you could couch as you go, laying out your yarn or heavy thread and sewing it down with invisible thread on your machine in the same step. For free-form couching, that is great, but for stained glass couching, I prefer to glue baste my couching fiber into place first to make sure it is exactly where I want it, and then go back and sew it down.

Here are two good rules of thumb:

• The smaller the scale of the block, the finer the couching fiber should be.

• It is always best to glue baste the shortest seams into place first, using a large-eyed chenille needle to bring any ends within the block to the back. This approach keeps things tidy. Then proceed with the longer seams.

## Tools and Supplies

For this example I used ⅛" metallic ribbon, a chenille #18 needle, a ruler, Roxanne Glue-Baste-It in a squeeze bottle with a fine-tip applicator, smoke-colored invisible thread, fine bobbin thread, a 70/10 machine needle, scissors, an iron, my sewing machine, the pieced quilt block, fusible interfacing cut to the size of the block, and a damp paper towel.

## Step by Step

Follow the instructions for this example when you try it yourself.

1. Stabilize the block with a lightweight fusible interfacing, following the manufacturer's instructions. This helps keep the seamlines within the block from wiggling and makes your zigzag sewing go more smoothly.

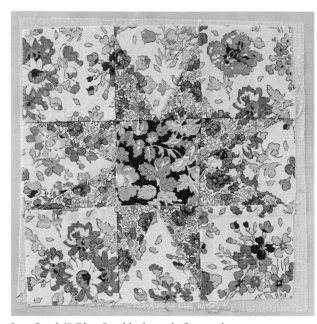

Interfaced 6″ Ohio Star block, ready for couching

2. Bring your first short couching thread to the front from the back at the apex of an inner triangle, using the large needle. Leave a 1″ tail on the back.

3. Use a ruler to apply the glue along the ditch between the patches. It gives a straight line and keeps your hand steady. Keep a damp paper towel handy to wipe off the ruler as needed.

4. Press the leading gently into place with your fingertips. You can make subtle adjustments at this stage if your line isn't quite straight, using the ruler to guide you.

5. After the couching fibers along the 4 triangle inner seams have been glue basted, lay the couching fiber along the longer seams. As in Steps 3 and 4, glue a straight line using the ruler's edge and then press the couching fiber into place. Extend the ends 1″ beyond the edges of the block, to be trimmed later.

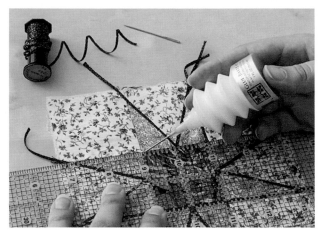

Apply a line of glue along a long seam, using a ruler.

6. When all the seams are covered, gently press the block with an iron (do not scrub) to make sure all is flat. This helps set the glue as well—but you can still pull up the couching fiber and reglue it into position if need be.

7. Thread your machine with the invisible thread on top and fill a bobbin with lightweight thread that matches the color of the couching fiber.

> **Tip**
>
> *Make a sample of a few glued couched fibers on a piece of interfaced fabric. Zigzag stitch the couching fiber into place, checking your machine's tension and stitch width. I always set my stitch length to 1.5, but your machine may vary. The stitches should reach just outside the edges of the couched fiber. It is always good to start on a sample before committing to your block or project.*

8. Zigzag stitch the couched fibers into place. When finished, clip any invisible thread "whiskers" from the front, turn the block over, and clip off excess bobbin thread and couching fiber.

## Now You Try It

You surely must have some orphan blocks lying around, or perhaps some extra vintage blocks? If not, make some simple Nine-Patch blocks just so you have some seams to couch. Follow the above Steps 1–8. If you couch more than two blocks, couch the seam between the blocks after you sew them together.

Sewn couching

# *Appliquéd Ribbon and Trim Leading on Pieced Blocks*

This process is similar to couching, with the leading first glue basted into place and then sewn down using a zigzag stitch. But there are some important differences:

• The sequence of appliquéing ribbon is specifically determined so that the unfinished end of one ribbon is covered by its adjacent perpendicular ribbon. (See *Mondrian's Window*, page 68, and *Window for Frank*, page 78.)

Detail of *Mondrian's Window*

Detail of *Window for Frank*

But if the ribbons travel just across the block, this isn't necessary, as their ends will be finished in the seams between the blocks. (See *Windy Sunshine*, page 53.)

Detail of *Windy Sunshine*

• Sometimes it is just easier to run a line of glue down the length of the ribbon, rather than in the ditch between the glass fabric shapes. This technique can also be helpful when appliquéing ribbon within a large fabric shape, as with the triangles in *Window for Frank*, page 78.

Detail of *Window for Frank*

• I like to glue down all the ribbon leading first and then sew it all down at once.

• Any ribbon wider than ⅛″ needs to be zigzagged into place on both sides, rather than in one pass with stitching going across the whole ribbon. It looks better that way.

• Blocks or large sections of a quilt pieced with wiggly fabrics—such as the cotton/silk blend used in the examples that follow—need to be stabilized before the ribbon is appliquéd. My favorite solution, especially for larger blocks, is to cut a piece of muslin to the size of the block, and machine baste all the seams in-the-ditch to the muslin—these will be covered by the ribbon. I also baste across the corners to hold everything in place, removing those stitches later. This is how *Mondrian's Window* (page 68) was constructed. Believe me, this step is well worth it. We want control here!

## Tools and Supplies

For this example I used ⅛″, ⅜″, and ⅞″ black velvet ribbon; a ruler; Roxanne Glue-Baste-It in a squeeze bottle with a fine-tip applicator; smoke-colored invisible thread; fine bobbin thread; a 70/10 machine needle; scissors; an iron; my sewing machine; the pieced quilt block; muslin cut to the size of the block; and a damp paper towel.

## Step by Step

1. Cut a piece of muslin slightly larger than the block. Press the block as flat as you can, with seam allowances pressed toward the darker fabrics. Then layer the block over the muslin.

2. Machine baste in-the-ditch along all seams and at the corners of the block. Press the block again.

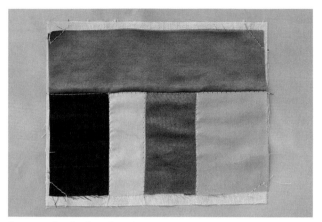

Baste in-the-ditch and at the corners.

3. Cut the short ribbon pieces to length. Use a ruler to run a line of glue along the ditch where the first short piece of ribbon will be placed, and then finger-press the ribbon into place on top of the glue line. Wipe down the ruler edge with a damp paper towel. Repeat for the other short pieces.

4. Using the ruler as a guide, run a line of glue along the back of the long piece of ribbon.

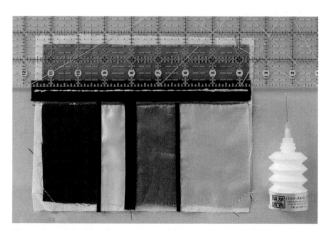

Steps 3 and 4: Glue baste short ribbons into place. Use a ruler to draw a line of glue on the back of the long ribbon.

5. Use the ruler to help you lay out the long ribbon in a straight line along its ditch, making sure it is perpendicular to the short pieces of ribbon. All the raw edges of the short ribbon pieces within the block are now covered. Turn the block over and press. This sets and dries the glue. Do not press the ribbon from the front, as it will melt!

6. Sew down all the ribbons using a zigzag stitch, with smoke-colored invisible thread on top and black light-weight thread in the bobbin. Clip all threads, turn over, and press.

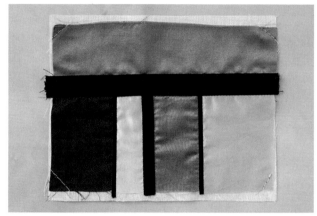

Finished block

## Now You Try It

Repeat the above Steps 1–6, using some old scraps of fabric, muslin, and either velvet ribbon or any narrow trim you have on hand. This is truly for practice so that you get familiar with working with the ruler, glue, and invisible zigzag stitching.

## Bonus: Rickrack as Leading

Black rickrack trim makes a whimsical leading that lends itself well to vintage 1930s quilt blocks. Varying the width from narrow to medium to wide rickrack in different areas of the quilt lends wonderful dynamism to the look, just as with the velvet ribbon. You can even use wide rickrack as a faux visual "binding" (see the example that follows).

Rickrack can be appliquéd as described above, although it benefits from a line of glue dots to tack it into place, rather than a solid line of glue in the ditch. All the other techniques apply.

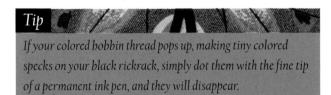

**Tip**

*If your colored bobbin thread pops up, making tiny colored specks on your black rickrack, simply dot them with the fine tip of a permanent ink pen, and they will disappear.*

*Vintage Pink*, 18″ × 18″, 2015

Made with vintage blocks

In this example, you can see I have chosen not to apply the rickrack between the four blocks or around all the little hexies. This lets me emphasize the pattern formed by the Ohio Star blocks. So as always, design options are many!

# Iron-On Bias Leading

This is the most accessible type of leading because all you need to create it are simple quilt fabrics and tools. It is the most versatile, too, because you can achieve such a variety of looks and widths, depending on which kind of fabric you use and how thin you slice it on the bias.

This is the basic concept: Glass fabrics are laid out on a foundation fabric, collage style. I don't fuse them on because I like to be able to reposition them as I am working, so I use either a fabric glue stick or temporary fabric adhesive spray to keep them in place (and flat) as I make the collage. Then I iron on the leading around those shapes. Because it is cut on the bias, this leading goes around curved shapes very well.

The fusible on the back of the leading fabric prevents it from fraying as long as you handle it gently. Sewing it down protects the leading's edges even more.

Sometimes the foundation fabric shows and is part of the design; sometimes the foundation is muslin and completely covered. Either way, after the collage is in place and leaded, all is zigzag stitched into place.

With this one technique you can create many different styles of traditional and contemporary stained glass quilt wallhangings (*The Parrish Farm*, page 43, and *Modern Rose Window*, page 44), as well as functional bed quilts (*Leaf Vine*, page 60). You can go further afield in your design choices, too, by letting the leading itself become a design element without surrounding any glass pieces (*Turkey in the Corn*, page 11, and *Fancy Autumn Vine*, page 67).

Finally, you have the option of sewing down the leading and quilting the quilt in the same step. On small, detailed pieces, where the added element of quilting designs is not needed, this is an excellent choice.

# Tools and Supplies

For this example I used foundation fabric; glass fabric scraps; a small, lightweight iron; a fabric glue stick; sharp fabric-cutting scissors; tracing paper; paper scissors; a pencil; and a temporary fabric marking pen (optional).

For leading I used fabric, fusible web (I prefer the lightest weight, either Mistyfuse or SoftFuse), a lightweight small iron, a ruler, a cutting mat and rotary cutter, sharp-pointed embroidery scissors, invisible thread for the top and lightweight bobbin thread, and a 60/8 or 70/10 machine needle.

# Step by Step

Let's start by showing how the leading is ironed on in straight lines and curves. Then we'll demonstrate how to make sharp points and square corners.

## Make the Leading Strips

1. Cut a 12″ × 12″ piece of black solid cotton and a 12″ × 12″ piece of fusible web. Following the manufacturer's instructions, fuse the web to the black cotton.

2. On the cutting mat, place the ruler diagonally across the square of fused fabric and cut from corner to corner. Put aside half of the fabric.

3. Place the ruler on the fabric along the bias-cut (diagonal) edge, with ¼″ of the fabric showing beyond the edge of the ruler. Cut. Reposition the ruler each time and continue cutting to make several ¼″ strips.

4. Repeat Step 3, making ⅛″-wide strips and then a few that are ⅜″ wide.

Fused black cotton leading fabric, showing front and back, cut on the bias into different widths

## Iron the Leading to the Background

1. Cut an 8″ × 8″ square of practice foundation fabric.

2. Holding the leading strip about 1″ from the end you are going to iron, use the tip of your iron to fuse the strip down onto the practice square.

3. Guide the leading into place with your left hand, following right along behind it with the tip of your iron.

4. Try straight lines and then a few curves, clipping off the leading where you wish it to stop.

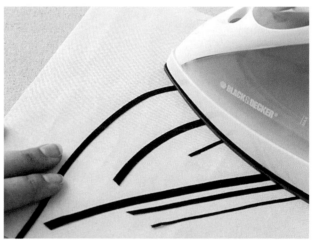

Steps 2–4: Iron on leading in a curve.

5. **Now create a corner** by fusing a strip and then overlapping a second strip at a right angle to make the corner. You will see that cutting the ends of the strips at a precise 90° angle will give you a beautifully square corner!

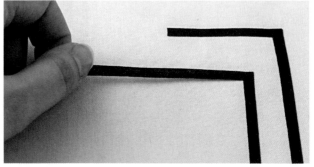

Hold leading in place to iron a corner.

6. **Make a sharp point** by cutting the ends of the leading at a sharp angle.

Clip leading at an angle to make a sharp point.

7. **Mark and then iron down a circle** of the leading. Finish by overlapping an end of the leading over the place where you started; iron and clip at an angle.

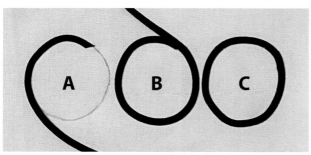

**A:** Begin to iron down the circle. **B:** Complete the circle by cutting the overlapped end at an angle. **C:** Completed circle

8. **Outline an image on printed fabric**, using the basic instructions in Steps 1–7. Be mindful of clipping the leading at the correct angle to achieve the corners you want. Note the thinner leading used to cover the antennae.

Printed butterfly being leaded

Completed leaded butterfly. For a detailed version of this same process, see *Vintage Wholecloth Stained Glass* (page 45).

## Now You Try It

Use the guide and patterns below to create this simple vine and leaves sample to help you practice the basics of iron-on bias leading.

Simple vine guide

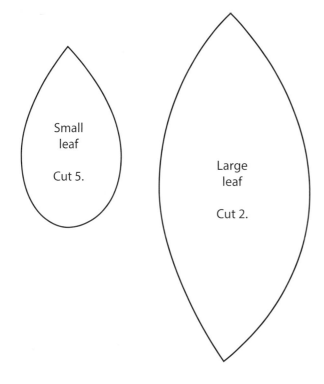

Small leaf

Cut 5.

Large leaf

Cut 2.

## Make and Arrange the Pieces

Refer to Iron-On Bias Leading, under Tools and Supplies (page 37), to gather what you will need.

1. Follow Make the Leading Strips, Steps 1–4 (page 37).

2. Create the leaf shapes in 1 of 2 ways: Trace around the leaf shapes with tracing paper. Cut out the paper templates with paper scissors, use to mark leaf fabric, and cut out the shapes. There is no seam allowance, so cut on the marked line.

*or*

Use the leaf shapes as a visual guide, and cut out free-form leaves. Just make sure the shapes are simple.

3. Using the diagram as a guide, mark the 2 stems on the foundation square.

4. Using the ¼″ leading, first press on the short stem and then press on a slightly wider strip for the long stem, clipping the leading off at the ends of the marked lines.

5. Dot the back of each leaf with the glue stick and position it into place on the foundation fabric, according to the diagram, being sure to cover the tops of the 2 stems with small leaves. Press the collage flat.

6. Gently press down a ⅛″ strip at the tip of the first small leaf. Curve the leading around the round bottom end of the leaf and then up the other side. Clip it off at the proper angle to get a sharp point when you get back to the tip.

7. For the larger leaf, press on the leading covering an edge, again clipping at the proper angle to create the sharp point. Repeat for the other edge.

8. Press on the leading for the remaining leaves.

9. Turn the collage over and press it very flat. You are now ready to sew the leading down.

The simple vine in progress

### Tips

#### Iron-On Leading

- *Remember, when applying iron-on leading, do not stretch it! Just gently guide it around the shape with one hand, ironing it in place right behind with the other hand.*

- *To get a sharp point at the tip of the leaf, begin at the base and end at the tip. That way you can clip the leading at the precise angle you need to make that sharp point.*

- *Make sure the leaf edges are trimmed as cleanly as possible before you apply the leading, which you can do even after the leaves are glued into place if need be. Keep a little piece of masking tape on hand for "blotting" any thread or leading flecks from your work surface before you apply the leading.*

- *If some leading gets wrinkled as you press it on, gently press your work from the back to try to relax it so that it is flat again. If you can't, you can press a new piece of leading over the problem spot. It won't show.*

## Sew Down the Leading

Simple vine, sewn down and quilted in the same step. Add more quilting if you wish.

For a very detailed version of this same process, see *Fern Vine* (page 67).

As you can see, the design has been layered over the batting and backing fabric. Sewing down the leading with a zigzag stitch functions as quilting in the same step. This is easy on a small piece; on a large bed quilt, such as *Leaf Vine* (page 60), it is impractical. Those leaves are zigzagged first and the quilt top is completely assembled. Then the completed top, batting, and backing fabric are sandwiched and quilted.

### Tips

### Stitching the Leading

- *Invisible thread is best for zigzagging. If you stitch into the background fabric while you are sewing down the leading, the thread won't show up so much. Use a lightweight thread in the bobbin.*

- *Always start with a little practice sample sandwich to make sure your tension and stitch width are just right. On my machine, invisible thread requires a looser tension, but every machine is different.*

- *Using a fine needle minimizes any holes in the fabric (important when using some silks and other delicate fabrics).*

- *Ideally, the width of the zigzag stitch will just cover the width of the leading. The exception is when the leading is quite wide, such as the stems in the collage. Wide leading is sewn down on each side with a narrow zigzag.*

- *If the leading changes widths even a tiny bit, you can change the width of the zigzag along the way to match it, width for width. (Stop sewing first, though.)*

- *I personally don't bother clipping my bobbin threads as I start and stop, repositioning my work as I sew. I go back and clip them all off at the end.*

- *Do sew slowly, with your needle set in the down position when you stop the machine. That makes pivoting and changing directions simple.*

- *Wearing a quilting glove on your left hand truly helps you to move the work around as you sew. I never sew without it.*

- *If your machine has a knee-lift to raise and lower the presser foot, use it as you sew. It makes all the changing of directions much easier.*

# Gallery

These quilts all show different ways to use the leading and quilt construction techniques from Chapters Two and Three. I hope you will find lots of visual information here that will give you plenty of your own ideas to try. I deeply enjoyed making these quilts.

***The Parrish Farm***    21″ × 32″

Detail of *The Parrish Farm*. The leading is as narrow as ¹⁄₂₄″.

***Modern Rose Window***   39½″ × 39½″

Leading doesn't always have to be black. Inspired by the Modern Quilt movement, this quilt aims for a simple and contemporary take on the symmetrical rose window with green cotton leading, simple solid shapes, and a white background. For a more traditional look, see *Silk Rose Window* (page 10). Note that the leading is used to suggest grillwork between the flowers.

### *Vintage Wholecloth Stained Glass*   30½″ × 30½″

You can outline the elements within a large printed panel, again using varying widths of iron-on leading, to give it a stained glass effect. A basic rule of thumb I used was the larger the element within the panel, the thicker the leading. Once the leading was on, all was sewn down and quilted in the same step, with more quilting added in the border. See the border of *Henri's Window* (page 9) and the detail of *Henri's Window* (page 30) to see other large prints outlined with a uniform-width leading.

Detail of *Vintage Wholecloth Stained Glass*. All this took was time and patience!

***Easter Sunrise***   18″ × 23″

Silver lamé was used for the iron-on leading. The window is set into stonelike hand-painted fabric that evokes an old wall.

**Love Wreath**  19″ × 20″

This variation of *Welcome Wreath* (page 83) uses hand-dyed wool as the glass fabric. The iron-on leading is made of silk/Lycra knit. The leading was also used to make the letters. It was quilted and appliquéd in one step, with echo quilting added afterwards.

***Sunrise for Frances***   16″ × 25″

Frances Holliday Alford hand dyed the sky and lake fabric, which is why this quilt is for her. Couched gold thread surrounds the cut-up trim used for the leaves as well as the cut-out printed flowers. Gold trim was appliquéd for the wider leading. This is the only quilt that has any three-dimensional embellishments, which are not normally included on a stained glass quilt, but they had to be there. Rules can be stretched!

**Stained Glass Wheels**  58″ × 74″

I couched dense black yarn in the ditch of most of the seams of these vintage Carpenter's Wheel blocks to give the quilt a contemporary stained glass edge. Adding the border increased this quilt enough in size to make it functional. It was quilted by Holly Casey.

***Michigan Robin***   19″ × 25″

When my friend Dale Kastle offered to send me a machine-embroidered bird (from the Embroidery Library, emblibrary.com) I was excited to see how I could incorporate my home state bird into a stained glass quilt. In this example the leading is couched perle cotton #3 around the hand-painted border flowers; gimp trim and the perle cotton separate the main sections of the quilt. The appliquéd apple blossoms in the border mimic the flowers in the print—the Michigan state flower, of course!

**_Tessie Bird_**   9¼″ × 11¼″

My second cousin, Tess Hall Neri, designs and makes mosaics and graciously allowed me to use this bird from one of her pieces. Instead of rotary cutting the iron-on leading, I cut it freehand with scissors to look a little more like grout. This piece was quilted and appliquéd in the same step.

# 4 Work Flow and Good Habits

At last we are ready to begin a project. To ensure success, set up your table for a smooth work flow and practice good work habits. This will support your best efforts and make these stained glass quilting techniques so enjoyable.

What follows is a distillation of my experience in how I set up my work space and the habits I have formed to keep the process flowing smoothly.

## The Worktable

• You need a cutting mat and an ironing surface adjacent to each other on your worktable. You need to be able to slice leading as you need it while working, even if you have a pile of it already prepared.

• A large piece of wool, folded in half to make two layers, is an ideal surface for ironing the leading onto the collage. Having it right next to, *but not on*, the cutting mat on the same table is perfect. You can also use cotton knit fleece, with the smooth knit side up, as a good ironing surface.

• Keep a piece of newspaper on hand for when you need to use the glue stick on the back of the glass pieces. The newspaper protects your cutting mat when you glue. Keep it at the top end of your cutting mat, and change it often because it gets sticky.

• Run a lint roller over the cutting mat to pick up bits and threads.

• If you have room, use an area of your table for arranging the fabrics you will be using, so you can see them at a glance. Otherwise, just bring a chair over and pile them up there. The point is, they need to be close at hand.

• The sewing machine belongs at the far end of the table. Turn it sideways to make more room when you are not using it.

• Switch up work areas as needed. When a collage is ready for sewing, remove the cutting mat and ironing station, so you have a clean and unobstructed surface on the table while sewing.

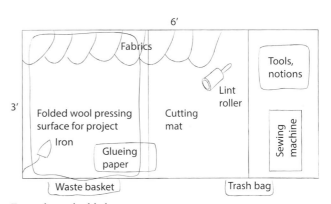

Example worktable layout

## Keep Things Tidy

This may sound obvious, but it is still good to remember:

• Keep your work space clean. Tape a small trash bag to the edge of your table for bits, and have a waste-basket right under the table. Tidy up the clutter at the end of each work session so you can really see what you are doing.

• Keep your hands clean. A peanut butter sandwich can cause disaster if you don't wash up before working!

• Use good tools: sharp scissors, a new rotary blade, fresh needles in your machine, a clean iron. These make all the difference.

# Windy Sunshine

### Finished block: 7½˝ × 7½˝  ●  Finished quilt: 47˝ × 62˝

*Glass and leading techniques: Glue appliqué (page 55), appliquéd ribbon (page 33), couching (page 31)*

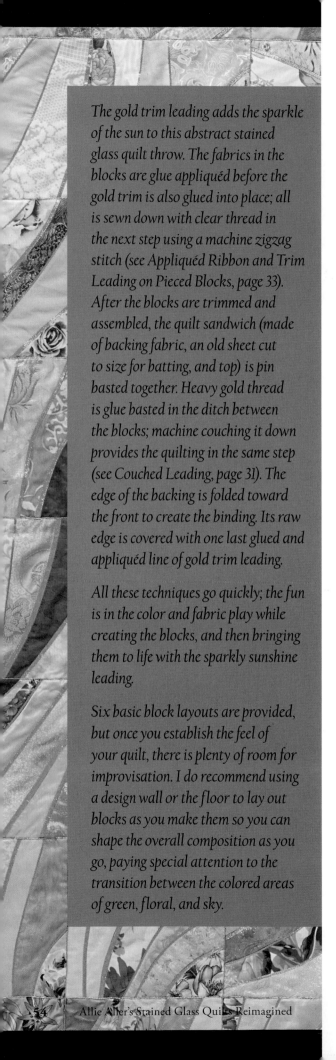

The gold trim leading adds the sparkle of the sun to this abstract stained glass quilt throw. The fabrics in the blocks are glue appliquéd before the gold trim is also glued into place; all is sewn down with clear thread in the next step using a machine zigzag stitch (see Appliquéd Ribbon and Trim Leading on Pieced Blocks, page 33). After the blocks are trimmed and assembled, the quilt sandwich (made of backing fabric, an old sheet cut to size for batting, and top) is pin basted together. Heavy gold thread is glue basted in the ditch between the blocks; machine couching it down provides the quilting in the same step (see Couched Leading, page 31). The edge of the backing is folded toward the front to create the binding. Its raw edge is covered with one last glued and appliquéd line of gold trim leading.

All these techniques go quickly; the fun is in the color and fabric play while creating the blocks, and then bringing them to life with the sparkly sunshine leading.

Six basic block layouts are provided, but once you establish the feel of your quilt, there is plenty of room for improvisation. I do recommend using a design wall or the floor to lay out blocks as you make them so you can shape the overall composition as you go, paying special attention to the transition between the colored areas of green, floral, and sky.

## MATERIALS

*Yardage is based on 42"-wide fabric, unless otherwise noted.*

**Muslin:** 37"/38" wide, 3⅛ yards for block foundations

**Garden greens, florals (solids and prints), and sky blues / lavenders:** Scraps, 4 yards total (These can be cotton, silk, polyester, and linen in solids, hand-dyeds, jacquards, and prints.)

**Backing:** 3 yards (The edge of the backing will be folded to the front to form the binding, so make sure the fabric is one you want to see on the front.)

**Thin batting:** 52" × 70" (I used an old twin flat sheet.)

**Flat gold trim:**

• ⅛", ¼", and ⅜" wide—20 yards each—for a total of 60 yards, for leading (This is inexpensive and can be found in the bridal section of any fabric store.)

• ⅝" wide, 6⅛ yards for binding edge

### Notions and Tools

**Thread:**

• Clear monofilament thread for top

• Neutral 50-weight thread for bobbin

• Gold braid-type thread #16, 2 spools (20 m total), for couching (Kreinik is a good brand; see A Few of My Favorite Supplies, page 98.)

**Needles:** 70/10 universal machine needles

**Fabric glue** (with fine-tip applicator)

**Temporary fabric marking pen**

**Large fabric scissors**

**Paper scissors:** For cutting gold trim (The trim will dull your good fabric scissors.)

**24" ruler**

**Optional:** Spray starch

# Construction

*Seam allowances are ¼" unless otherwise noted.*

## Make the Blocks

> **NOTE:** *I advise making a few practice blocks before you dive in. This will give you a feel for the techniques and sewing involved, and you will discover how simple and easy this method is.*

1. From the muslin, cut 48 squares 8½" × 8½" for the foundation squares.

> **NOTE:** *Though the blocks will finish at 7½" × 7½", the extra margin is important for ease in trimming the blocks later. This is the voice of experience speaking!*

2. Assemble the scraps into 3 piles: garden greens, florals (prints and solids), and sky blues / lavenders.

3. Using the block diagrams as a guide, mark the first foundation square with the fabric pen in gentle curves. The block should have between 5 and 8 curved shapes. These block designs may be flipped and rotated for further variation. Continue marking all 48 muslin squares, using the full variety of block diagrams. Remember, it is okay to change your mind later, but marking the foundations and putting them up on the wall now gives a good sense of how the design will flow across the quilt.

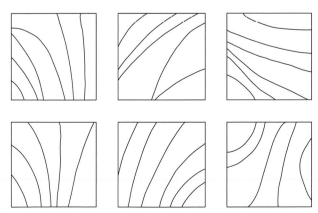

Six block layout options

### The Glue Appliqué Method

Your workstation should have an ironing surface—a large folded piece of wool works well—and a gluing area beside your sewing machine.

1. Referring to the quilt photo (page 53), look at the top left block as Block 1. Arrange the muslin squares in your desired order on the design wall in 8 rows of 6 blocks.

2. For Block 1 (top left corner of the quilt layout), choose the fabrics for the shapes, referring to the quilt photo for color guidance. Rough cut each shape to be slightly larger than what the finished sewn-down shapes will be on the block (the grain doesn't matter). Lay out the pieces on the foundation to make sure you like them, and then arrange them next to the foundation square.

3. Starting with the shape for the lower right corner of the block, put a dab of glue on the back of the piece and lay it down on the block foundation.

Starting a block with the glue appliqué method. These colors show the transition between the garden greens and the floral fabrics.

4. Fold under the edge of the second shape where it will overlap the first shape, creating a scant ¼″ seam allowance, and press. It helps to give the edge a spritz of spray starch after you press it under the first time, and then press it again.

5. Run a line of glue along the folded edge, and then finger-press the shape into place on the block, overlapping the raw edge of the first shape. Next, press it into place with your iron. This sets the glue and gives you a perfectly flat edge. (It is easy to pull up the patch after it has been pressed if need be, however.)

6. Add the leading by applying a line of glue to the back of a piece of flat gold trim and then finger-pressing it into place between 2 fabric shapes. Gently press over the trim to set the glue.

> **NOTE:** *Because both ends of the trim extend off the block, you don't have to worry about finishing their ends. They will be encased in the seams between the blocks.*

Glue the first piece of gold trim leading.

7. Continue spray starching and pressing the seam allowances under, applying the glue, and adding the shapes in place until the foundation square is covered and all the leading is added. Use a variety of widths of flat gold trim as desired—this adds a dynamic look.

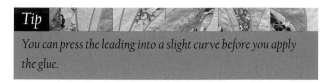

**Tip**
*You can press the leading into a slight curve before you apply the glue.*

8. When all the leading is in place, appliqué it down using a wide zigzag over the entire ⅛″ trim, or a narrow zigzag on each side of the wider trims. Make sure you catch the fabrics on each side of the trim with your zigzag, as this stitching is appliquéing the blocks at the same time it is stitching the leading.

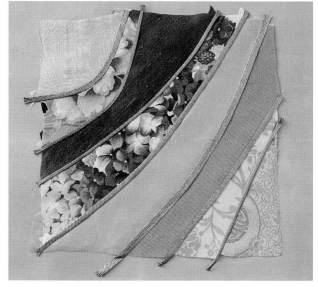

The block is all glued down and ready for sewing with clear thread using a zigzag stitch.

9. Trim the block to 8″ × 8″. As a final step, stitch around the perimeter of the trimmed block using a narrow zigzag. This step will prevent fraying as the block is handled. Place the block on the design wall in its appropriate position.

10. Repeat Steps 2–9 for the rest of the blocks, placing them on the design wall to help you make color selections from block to block.

Completed and trimmed block

## Assemble the Quilt Top

1. Start with the bottom row of blocks and sew all 6 blocks together using a scant ¼″ seam allowance.

2. Press the seams open between the blocks. This will make the couching/quilting step go smoothly and give a better finished look to the quilt. Use the end of a seam ripper or stiletto to gently open the seam allowances so you can finger-press them open before you iron them. This is picky work, but worth it. A light spritz of water from a spray bottle onto the seam allowances helps flatten them out as you press them open with your iron.

3. Assemble all 8 rows this way, and then sew the rows together. Again, press the seams between the rows open.

## Assemble the Quilt

I used an old fitted twin sheet from when my son was little, cut to size for my batting. (Or you can find a cheap one at a thrift shop.) This is a good choice for a light-weight throw with minimal quilting.

Both layers will be folded over to become the binding.

1. Sew the quilt backing fabric to create a piece 55″ × 70″. Cut the sheet batting the same size. Layer the backing right side down with the sheet on top of it. Then center the quilt top over the sheet. Pin baste the layers together.

2. Measure and mark the backing and batting exactly 2″ beyond each side of the quilt top. Trim the sandwiched backing and batting sheet along marked line, using long-bladed scissors. This outer edge of backing/batting will become the 1″ binding.

### Add the Couching/Quilting

Use a metallic braid #16 from Kreinik (see A Few of My Favorite Supplies, page 98) or any heavy gold thread that will work. You will be couching it down in the ditch between the blocks. (See Couched Leading, page 31.)

1. Starting between the bottom 2 rows of blocks, run a fine line of glue in the ditch all the way across the quilt.

2. Lay and finger-press the braid into the ditch. The glue will hold it in place for sewing.

3. Set your machine to a narrow zigzag and sew over the braid, clipping it just past the edge of the quilt top. You are quilting the layers together in this same step.

4. Repeat with all remaining horizontal rows, sewing down each line of couching fiber after it has been glue basted into place. Then turn the quilt, and glue baste and couch/quilt the vertical rows. The throw is now ready for binding.

A detail showing the couched heavy gold thread—which also functions as the quilting

## Bind and Label Your Quilt

This binding has mitered corners and a beautiful finished edge. Follow the series of photos to see how these are accomplished.

1. Fold the corner of the backing/batting layers at 45° until the tip of the triangle meets the corner of the quilt top. Press.

Fold the backing/batting to form a triangle.

2. Now fold and press the edge of the backing/batting to the edge of the quilt top. Repeat with the adjacent side, forming a miter in the corner.

One side has been pressed, showing how the miter is formed.

3. Machine zigzag the raw edge of the binding all the way around the quilt. Go back and sew the miters closed by hand.

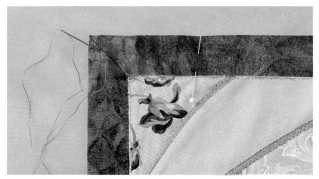

One side is zigzagged, and the miter is being sewn closed.

4. Starting at the bottom center of the quilt, run a line of glue precisely over the center of the zigzagged raw edge.

5. Finger-press the ⅝″ gold trim into place over the glue. When you get to the corner, simply fold a miter into the trim, press, and pin.

6. Repeat Steps 4 and 5 until you have gone all the way around the quilt with the gold trim. Fold over ½″ at the end of the trim to hide the raw edge where you started.

7. Appliqué with a narrow zigzag and clear thread on each side of the ⅝″ gold trim leading.

8. Appliqué the mitered gold trim corners closed by hand.

Corner, showing the finished binding

9. As always, make a label with your name, the date, where you made the quilt, and for what occasion. Give your work the documentation it deserves!

# A Variation

These blocks show the same glue-appliquéd leading technique and block layouts, but in an alternative color scheme with iron-on leading. So do you see that this project can be interpreted in many ways? How will you make it?

An alternative colorway for the Windy Sunshine blocks

# Leaf Vine

**Finished vertical strips:** 14˝ × 90˝ ● **Finished quilt:** 72˝ × 90˝

*Leading technique: Iron-on leading (page 36)*

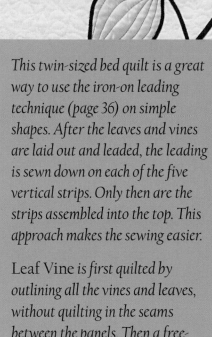

This twin-sized bed quilt is a great way to use the iron-on leading technique (page 36) on simple shapes. After the leaves and vines are laid out and leaded, the leading is sewn down on each of the five vertical strips. Only then are the strips assembled into the top. This approach makes the sewing easier.

Leaf Vine is first quilted by outlining all the vines and leaves, without quilting in the seams between the panels. Then a free-motion allover leaf pattern is quilted in the open white spaces.

It's a great scrap buster since you can use just one color, as I have, or go multicolored. And though the main vine placement is roughly the same on all five strips, there is plenty of scope for improvisation in the leaf placement. Look at the layout diagram (page 61) to get the idea, and then take it from there.

## MATERIALS

*Yardage is based on 42"-wide fabric, unless otherwise noted.*

**White fabric:** 5⅛ yards for background strips

**Green scraps:** Approximately 3 yards (I used velvet, poly, silk, velveteen, brocade, hand-dyed cotton, vintage kimono silk, and cotton, but all cotton is fine.)

**Solid black cotton:** 1½ yards for leading

**Backing:** 5½ yards

**Binding:** Premade single-fold black cotton binding (or make your own), 10 yards

**Batting:** 80" × 98"

## Notions and Tools

**Lightweight fusible web:** 24" wide, 4 yards for leading

**Fabric marking pen or chalk**

**Glue stick or liquid fabric glue**

**Thread:**

- Smoke-colored invisible thread for top
- Black 50-weight thread for bobbin
- White quilting thread and bobbin thread

**Needles:**

- Size 70/10 universal machine needles
- Machine quilting needle of your choice

**Mini-iron**

**Sharp embroidery scissors**

**Cutting mat**

**Ruler** (at least 24" long)

**Rotary cutter**

**Tracing paper and card stock or template plastic**

**Masking tape**

This layout gives the overall plan; the individual placement of the leaves can be somewhat improvisational. The goal is to fill the space evenly with leaves. Each strip has around 60 leaves.

# CUTTING

## White Fabric

1. For the long foundation strips, cut the 5⅛ yards in half lengthwise to get 2 lengths about 2½+ yards each.

2. Cut 4 strips 15″ × 90″, 2 from each length.

3. Sew the remaining fabric pieces together along the long edges, using a ¼″ seam allowance. Press the seam open, and don't worry, this won't show on the finished quilt. Cut the fifth 15″ × 90″ strip from this piece.

## Green Scraps

1. Use the A, B, C, and D leaf patterns (next page) to prepare templates. Trace the leaf shapes onto tracing paper. Cut them out and lightly glue them to card stock. Cut them out again, and your templates are ready. Or you can trace them onto template plastic and cut them out.

2. Place the templates on the right side of your fabrics, tracing around them with a fabric pen or chalk (the latter works well on velvet and dark fabrics). You don't need to add a seam allowance to the templates. Cut out approximately 320 leaves in a variety of shapes.

> **NOTE:** *Remember to sometimes reverse the A and B leaf templates as you trace them onto the leaf fabrics so that you have more variety in the leaf shapes. If you wish to shade your vine from dark at the bottom to light at the top, as in the quilt shown, cut 80 of the leaves from the dark fabrics, 160 from the medium fabrics, and 80 from the light fabrics.*

## Set Up Your Worktable

Having an organized workstation is so helpful for ensuring a pleasant and successful experience with this technique. See the sample worktable layout (page 52) to set up your work surface.

A folded 1½-yard piece of wool makes a great ironing surface for ironing down the leading. Have a cutting mat nearby for cutting extra leading as needed and a small sheet of paper to use as a surface for gluing the leaves to protect your table. Keep the piles of leaves nearby, neatly organized into dark, medium, and light.

## Prepare the Leading

1. Cut fusible web to 17″ × 30″ lengths. (Fusible web usually comes off the roll at 17″ wide.) This is a good size for using a 24″ ruler at a 45° angle when making leading strips.

2. Following the manufacturer's instructions, fuse the fusible web to the back of the black fabric.

3. Cut 45° bias leading in strips (see Making the Leading Strips, page 37). This will provide some bias to make the strips easy to iron along a curve. You need big piles of ¼″ strips for the main vines and ³⁄₁₆″ strips for the leaves and their stems. You don't need to cut them all at once, though!

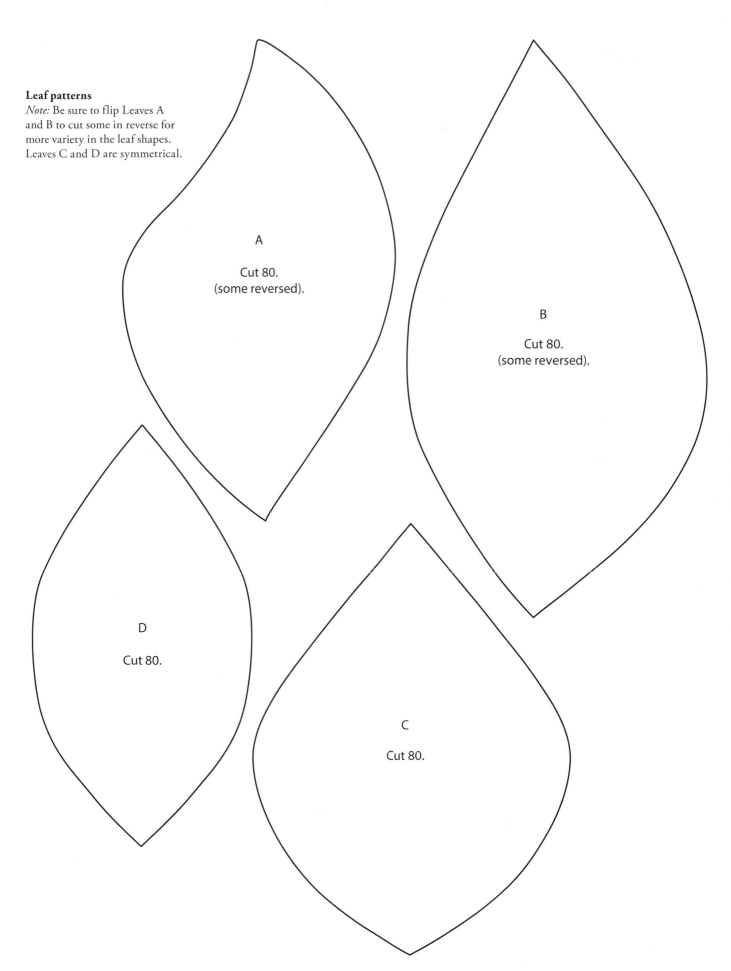

**Leaf patterns**
*Note:* Be sure to flip Leaves A and B to cut some in reverse for more variety in the leaf shapes. Leaves C and D are symmetrical.

A

Cut 80.
(some reversed).

B

Cut 80.
(some reversed).

D

Cut 80.

C

Cut 80.

# Create the Leaf Vine Strips

We will work through the first strip step by step, and then you will repeat the process four more times. I prefer laying out the entire quilt before sewing it all down.

A design wall or the floor is also helpful for being able to see the strips as you arrange them, so you can tweak the composition if need be.

## Vines and Stems

1. Referring to the diagram and using a temporary fabric marker, draw the main vine along the entire length of a 15″ × 90″ white strip.

2. Draw in the secondary stems.

3. Using your marking as a guide, fuse the 3/16″-wide secondary stems coming off the main vine first. Start at the outside of the secondary vines and gently press toward the marked main vine line. The bias of the leading will allow the strips to take those curves very nicely.

4. When the secondary vines reach the main vine line, clip the leading with sharp embroidery scissors so that the ends are parallel to the main vine line.

5. Use the 1/4″ leading for the main vine. Start at the top of the strip and place the end of the leading over the top of the marked main vine. Fuse the strip, following the marked line. When you need to add the next piece of leading, simply lap the beginning of the next piece 1/2″ over the end of the last piece.

6. Continue all the way down the main vine, covering the ends of the secondary shoots in the center as you go.

## Add the Leaves

1. Starting at the base of the vine, arrange leaves at the ends of the stems and on the main vine as inspired by the diagram. Work from dark greens upward through middle and light greens to the top, if desired. Trim leaves to tweak their shapes, if needed, along the way. Pin them into place; 1 or 2 pins per leaf is fine.

2. When you are happy with the arrangement, glue each leaf in place with a dot of glue stick or liquid fabric glue at each end of the leaf, removing the pins as you go. You don't need more glue than that. It is easy to reposition a leaf after it is lightly glued, should you change your mind.

3. After the leaves are glued down, take a length of 3/16″ leading and press it around the first leaf, using a separate piece of leading for each side of the leaf. You will be cutting each piece to size after it has been pressed in place, not before. It would be too hard to judge the correct length for each piece of leading beforehand! (See Now You Try It, page 40.)

4. Proceed up the vine, pressing the leading around each leaf.

5. Complete the next 4 strips in the same way.

Clipping the point at the tip of a leaf

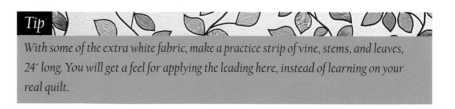

*Tip*

*With some of the extra white fabric, make a practice strip of vine, stems, and leaves, 24″ long. You will get a feel for applying the leading here, instead of learning on your real quilt.*

# Sew Down the Stems. Vines, and Leaves

## Some Points before You Start

1. Press the strip from the back to make sure all is as flat as possible before you begin sewing.

2. With a 50-weight or finer black thread in the bobbin, appliqué the leading using a 70/10 universal needle with smoke-colored invisible thread. Sew with a zigzag stitch set just wider than the width of the leading. (If your leading strips seem too wide for one pass of the zigzag, use a narrower stitch on either side of the leading strips. This is especially appropriate on the main vines.) I set a stitch length of 1.5 on my machine. You may need to experiment to find the perfect stitch length setting on your machine. The smoke-colored invisible thread disappears into the leading so much better than clear invisible thread!

> **Tip**
>
> *Practice on your sample to make sure the thread tension is right and the stitches are the correct width. A too-wide stitch will go out into the background fabric and show a little bit; too narrow and it will pinch the width of the leading, causing "tunneling." Your goal is a perfect, clean black line.*

3. Roll up the strips from the bottom so that you have a manageable sewing area, and just reroll the ends like a scroll as you sew down the long strip of leaves and vines. Work in 24″ sections.

## Sew the Leading

1. Starting at the top of the strip, appliqué the main vine first in a wide zigzag down 24″ or so.

2. Appliqué the leaves, turning your work as needed. I do not use free motion for this, as I want my zigzag perfectly consistent. (A walking foot is always good to use, if you have one. A knee-lift for the presser foot on your machine is very helpful, too.)

3. You will be starting and stopping often. At the end of a line of sewing, just sew a few extra zigzag stitches in place; clip the top thread at the surface and the bobbin from underneath. You can trim off the bobbin threads on the back later.

4. Proceed down the strip until all is sewn down. Turn the strip over and iron it flat once again.

5. Complete the remaining 4 strips in the same manner.

# Construct the Quilt

*Seam allowances are ¼" unless otherwise noted.*

## Assemble the Top and Backing Fabric

1. Sew the first 2 strips together. Make sure they are oriented correctly before you sew!

2. After sewing, press the seam open.

3. Repeat Steps 1 and 2 until all the strips are sewn together.

4. Cut the 5½ yards of backing in half to make 2 pieces 2¾ yards each. Sew them together lengthwise and then press the seam open.

## Quilt, Bind, and Label

Layer the top, batting, and backing. Quilt and bind as desired.

*Here Are My Quilting and Binding*

1. With invisible thread, I quilted in-the-ditch around all leaves, stems, and vines.

2. To make the leaves and vines stand out, I picked an overall pattern and closely quilted the background fabric. I used a free-motion little leaf pattern, in white thread, to strengthen the theme of the quilt without drawing attention away from the main design of the vines.

3. Using a very fine black thread, I quilted the interior of each leaf in simple lines radiating between its tip and its base.

4. I used 10 yards of premade 1¼" single-fold binding.

5. Make a label with your name, the date, and where you made the quilt.

Detail of leaf quilting

# Variations to Consider

Here, two small quilts demonstrate what happens if you switch up the leading, colors, and scale of the leaf vines. The techniques are almost exactly the same as used in this project, but the outcomes are so different! What variations can you think of?

*Fancy Autumn Vines, 18″ × 20″, 2015*

*Fern Vine, 23″ × 24″, 2015*

Gold bonded lamé leading is fused around warm-colored leaves on a deep blue background. The leading itself becomes a design element with its curlicues both inside and outside the leaf shapes. The background is densely quilted to make those leaves and tendrils pop out in bas relief fashion.

On this piece, the leaves and vines were all laid out, and then the quilt sandwich of batting and backing was spray basted into place. Sewing down the little leaves and quilting them was therefore accomplished in the same step. This made sense in such a finely detailed piece. Outer borders were added and machine quilted. The quilt was bound with vintage trim.

# Mondrian's Window

**Finished quilt:** 60″ × 72″

*Leading technique: Appliquéd ribbon (page 33)*

In this project I loved using a mix of cotton and shiny fabrics that suggest the reflectivity of glass, as in a real stained glass window. In my quilt I've stayed with solids, hand-dyed fabrics, and plaids, to honor the painter Piet Mondrian's geometric abstraction style of painting, the inspiration for my design.

The quilt is divided into eight sections. Each section is pieced and layered over a corresponding muslin foundation, and then secured with some basting in-the-ditch. The sections are then sewn together to make the top. There are diagrams and cutting lists for each section to show how the quilt is divided and pieced.

An optional step is to use the iron-on leading technique (page 36) to add very fine lines of leading between the squares of any plaid fabric, before sewing the plaid piece into its section. This is a very easy and effective way to get lots more detail for very little extra work. People will think you did a lot of very tiny piecing, but you didn't!

## Tips

### Tips for Plaids

*If you include some plaid pieces in your quilt, you can use the grid lines in the plaid as guides for very fine strips of iron-on leading. You will need a cutting area to make the black cotton leading strips, which are about 1/16˝ wide, and a surface for the ironing. You will zigzag them down in place when you are sewing down the rest of the leading. It is an extra step, but it looks really great. (See Making the Leading Strips, page 37.)*

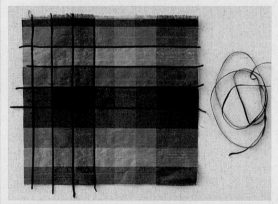

Some silk plaid in 1˝ squares with fine black cotton leading being ironed on to make a grid

Different thicknesses of leading—including leaded plaid—create a dynamic look.

Three different widths of black velvet ribbon are glued and then appliquéd over the seamlines to create the grid lines Mondrian was so famous for. Using the different widths really adds to the dynamic stained glass look of the quilt. Review the technique instructions for appliquéd ribbon and trim (page 33).

Finally, top, batting, and backing are pin basted, quilted, bound, and labeled.

## MATERIALS

*Yardage is based on 42"-wide fabric, unless otherwise noted.*

**Muslin:** 37"/38" wide, 5½ yards for backing pieced sections

**Brightly colored large solid and plaid scraps:** Approximately 5 yards (Silk and cotton/silk blends are great here, but solids or batiks work well too, as well as a few tone-on-tone hand-dyed fabrics.)

**Binding:** Premade single-fold black binding (or make your own), 8 yards

**Backing:** 3⅞ yards

**Batting:** 68" × 80"

**Optional:** 1 fat quarter (18" × 22") of black cotton and 1 fat quarter of fusible web for plaid leading

### Notions and Tools

**Black velvet ribbon:** (Ribbon yardages are approximate, with a little extra added.)

• ⅛" wide, 15 yards

• ⅜" wide, 20 yards

• ⅝" wide, 10 yards

**Thread:**

• Neutral piecing thread for top and bobbin

• Smoke-colored invisible thread for appliquéing ribbon and cotton leading

• Clear invisible thread for quilting

**Liquid fabric glue** (with a fine-tip applicator)

**Temporary fabric marking pen or pencil**

## CUTTING

### MUSLIN FOUNDATIONS

| Section | Cut size |
|---------|----------|
| Section A | 11" × 31" |
| Section B | 19" × 37½" |
| Section C | 19" × 26½" |
| Section D | 13" × 63" |
| Section E | 9" × 73" |
| Section F | 15" × 60½" |
| Section G | 9" × 60½" |
| Section H | 13½" × 23" |

*Tip*

*After cutting the muslin, write the letter of each section on the back.*

## Bright-Colored Glass Fabrics

Refer to the cutting charts for Sections A–H (next page). Find the dimensions for each piece and find its position in the quilt sections placement diagram (below). Label the cut piece with its letter/number. Just remember, the cutting size gives each piece a ½" seam allowance all the way around. (I prefer the ½" seam allowance because it gives me a little more leeway in this project for trimming up the sections, or in case I have to resew to make things fit better.)

I strongly recommend cutting out the pieces for a section at a time, as you work, not all at once.

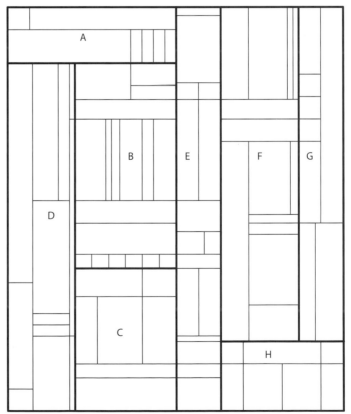

Quilt sections placement of the 8 main sections (A–H). Make a few enlarged copies of this diagram to use as coloring pages and to keep on your worktable for easy reference.

## CUTTING: SECTION A

| Piece | Cut size |
|-------|----------|
| A1 | 5″ × 5″ |
| A2 | 5″ × 27″ |
| A3 | 7″ × 23″ |
| A4 | 3″ × 7″ |
| A5 | 3″ × 7″ |
| A6 | 3″ × 7″ |
| A7 | 3″ × 7″ |

## CUTTING: SECTION C

| Piece | Cut size |
|-------|----------|
| C1 | 6″ × 13″ |
| C2 | 6″ × 7″ |
| C3 | 5″ × 13″ |
| C4 | 9″ × 13″ |
| C5 | 7″ × 13″ |
| C6 | 3½″ × 19″ |
| C7 | 7″ × 19″ |

## CUTTING: SECTION B

| Piece | Cut size |
|-------|----------|
| B1 | 5″ × 9″ |
| B2 | 3½″ × 9″ |
| B3 | 7½″ × 11″ |
| B4 | 4½″ × 19″ |
| B5 | 6½″ × 15½″ |
| B6 | 2″ × 15½″ |
| B7 | 2½″ × 15½″ |
| B8 | 5″ × 15½″ |
| B9 | 3″ × 15½″ |
| B10 | 5″ × 15½″ |
| B11 | 5″ × 19″ |
| B12 | 6½″ × 19″ |
| B13 | 3½″ × 4″ |
| B14 | 3½″ × 4″ |
| B15 | 3½″ × 4″ |
| B16 | 3½″ × 4″ |
| B17 | 3½″ × 4″ |
| B18 | 3½″ × 4″ |

## CUTTING: SECTION D

| Piece | Cut size |
|-------|----------|
| D1 | 5½″ × 40″ |
| D2 | 5½″ × 20″ |
| D3 | 5″ × 5½″ |
| D4 | 5½″ × 25½″ |
| D5 | 3″ × 25½″ |
| D6 | 7½″ × 21″ |
| D7 | 3″ × 7½″ |
| D8 | 3″ × 7½″ |
| D9 | 7½″ × 14½″ |
| D10 | 2″ × 11″ |
| D11 | 2″ × 39½″ |
| D12 | 2″ × 14½″ |

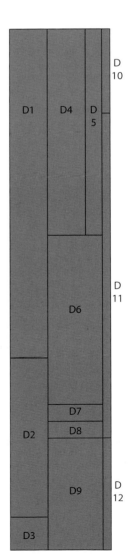

# CUTTING: SECTION E

| Piece | Cut size |
|-------|----------|
| E1 | 2½″ × 9″ |
| E2 | 9″ × 13″ |
| E3 | 4″ × 5″ |
| E4 | 4″ × 5″ |
| E5 | 5″ × 19″ |
| E6 | 5″ × 19″ |
| E7 | 6½″ × 9″ |
| E8 | 5″ × 6″ |
| E9 | 4″ × 5″ |
| E10 | 3½″ × 9″ |
| E11 | 5″ × 13″ |
| E12 | 5″ × 13″ |
| E13 | 2″ × 9″ |
| E14 | 5″ × 9″ |
| E15 | 3½″ × 9″ |
| E16 | 7″ × 9″ |

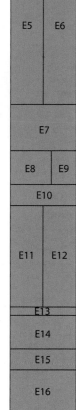

# CUTTING: SECTION F

| Piece | Cut size |
|-------|----------|
| F1 | 6″ × 17½″ |
| F2 | 8″ × 17½″ |
| F3 | 2″ × 17½″ |
| F4 | 2″ × 17½″ |
| F5 | 4½″ × 15″ |
| F6 | 5″ × 15″ |
| F7 | 8½″ × 14″ |
| F8 | 2½″ × 14″ |
| F9 | 2½″ × 10″ |
| F10 | 3″ × 10″ |
| F11 | 10″ × 13½″ |
| F12 | 7½″ × 10″ |
| F13 | 6″ × 36½″ |

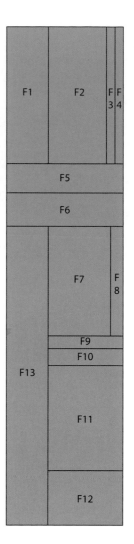

# CUTTING: SECTION G

| Piece | Cut size |
|-------|----------|
| G1 | 5″ × 13″ |
| G2 | 5″ × 5″ |
| G3 | 5″ × 5″ |
| G4 | 5″ × 5″ |
| G5 | 5″ × 15½″ |
| G6 | 5″ × 39½″ |
| G7 | 4″ × 22″ |
| G8 | 6″ × 22″ |

# CUTTING: SECTION H

| Piece | Cut size |
|-------|----------|
| H1 | 5″ × 5″ |
| H2 | 5″ × 15″ |
| H3 | 5″ × 5″ |
| H4 | 5″ × 9½″ |
| H5 | 8″ × 9½″ |
| H6 | 8″ × 9½″ |
| H7 | 5″ × 9½″ |

# Sew the Sections

*All seam allowances for this project are ½".*

Let's make Section A together so you can see how to approach the construction process. It is straight-line piecing; the twist is layering the pieced section over the corresponding muslin foundation and basting in-the-ditch. This will make appliquéing the ribbon so much easier. You need a stable base for those large areas of wiggly glass fabric. (Silk is notoriously wiggly.) Otherwise they will stretch and distort as you lay out and appliqué the velvet ribbon.

1. Refer to the Section A cutting chart and Section A diagram (page 71).

2. Cut out pieces A1 to A7. Remember, we are using a ½" seam allowance, included in the cutting measurements.

3. Sew together A1 and A2, and press the seams open.

4. Sew together A3, A4, A5, A6, and A7, and press the seams open.

5. Sew the A1-2 and A3-4-5-6-7 units together, and press the seams open.

6. Layer the pieced Section A over its corresponding muslin A piece. The pieced section should be the same size as the muslin piece. This is important so that the sections will go together easily.

7. Sew in-the-ditch with invisible thread along the main seams to attach the glass fabric section to the muslin. This will keep it from shifting as you are working with it later.

8. Use the basting stitch on your machine to make short lines of stay stitching at intervals around the perimeter of the section, barely inside the edge of the glass fabrics, just enough to tack everything into place and keep it flat.

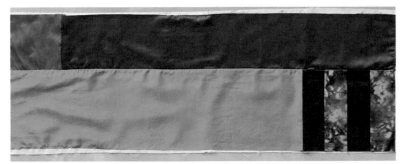

Section A is completed with all pieces pressed flat, the main seam stitched in-the-ditch, and the perimeter staystitched at intervals along each side. (The muslin shows in this example so you can see it; on your quilt, the edges of the section's glass and muslin layers will be flush.)

## Four Strategies for Your Quilt's Composition

- Make a few enlarged copies of the quilt sections placement diagram (page 70) and use them as a coloring book to try out color ideas.

- If you have a design wall, arrange the blank muslin foundation sections as they will be when assembled into the quilt top. Pin pieces in progress onto their corresponding muslin sections to see how they look. You can pin chunks of fabric in place on the adjacent sections, too, to audition them before cutting and sewing. You will see the quilt evolve as a whole this way.

- If you don't have a design wall, clear about a 5′ × 6′ space on the floor. Once the sections are all done, lay out the sections as they will be assembled into the quilt top. Because you can't leave them in place, snap digital photos to keep track of your ideas each time you arrange the sewn sections and audition fabrics. Then gather up the all the fabrics before the dog or the kids come through!

- Taking photos also helps you spot imbalances; they pop right out in a reduced-size image. Look at the image upside down, too, to make sure your composition looks good in both directions.

9. Refer to the Section A diagram (page 71) to mark an arrow on the muslin back so you know the correct orientation of Section A for the quilt layout.

10. Now that you have a feel for how this quilt will be put together, you can forge ahead. Repeat the process used in Section A for the remaining sections, B–H. Repeat Steps 6–9 to attach the appropriate muslin back to each section and mark each section with an arrow for orientation in the quilt. Have fun and make this quilt your own. The piecing is easy, but take your time. Be sure to measure twice before you cut! And just so you know, if a few corners don't line up in your sewing, the velvet ribbon will cover them. You can't tell where I used that trick, can you?

## NOTE:
### Keep in Mind While Working ...

- *As you work, you will no doubt generate some extra strips and squares. Keep them handy for improvisational sewing. You may find you wish to subdivide some of the sections into different geometric shapes than the ones shown. Improvisation can be fun here! You just want to keep the sections true to size so that they will fit together in the end.*

- *Make sure you press the seams really flat as you go along. Keep a little spritz bottle of water on your ironing table for this purpose.*

# Construct the Quilt

*All seam allowances for this project are ½".*

Refer to the quilt sequence diagram (below) to arrange the sections in the proper order. Double-check the marked section letters on the back of the muslin to make sure you are orienting the sections properly before you sew any sections together. Also, press the seams between sections open after each step. This will make the velvet ribbon lie flatter on the surface of the quilt.

1. Press and trim the edges of each section to the muslin size, cutting off any stray threads.

2. Sew together Sections B and C.

3. Sew Section B-C to Section D.

4. Sew Section B-C-D to Section A.

5. Sew together Sections F and G.

6. Sew Section F-G to Section H.

7. Sew Section A-B-C-D to Section E.

8. Sew Section A-B-C-D-E to Section F-G-H.

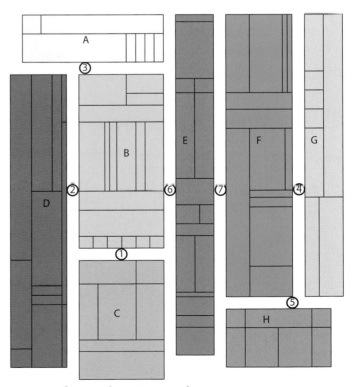

Sequence of sewing the sections together

# Add the Leading

Before you begin:

• Review Chapter Four (page 52) to set up your work space.

• Using three different widths of ribbon adds dynamism to the quilt, but truly the widths are chosen randomly—just don't outline all your sections in the widest ribbon.

• Make sure you apply short ribbons first and then cover their ends with the perpendicular longer pieces as you go.

• Don't press the front of the ribbon! It will melt. Always press the quilt from the back.

## Glue Appliqué the Leading

Refer to Appliquéd Ribbon and Trim Leading on Pieced Blocks (page 33). Here are some additional tips that are helpful when gluing long lengths of ribbon into place.

1. Center a long ruler lengthwise along the back of the ribbon. Run the line of glue onto the ribbon along the edge of the ruler, just as if you were using a rotary cutter. Keep a damp cloth on hand to wipe off the edge of the ruler after each pass.

2. Always use the ruler's edge as a guide when finger-pressing your ribbon into place. Put 2 rulers end to end for guiding and placing the long ribbons. This will ensure that your ribbon leading goes on straight.

3. As a final step, lay your clean see-through ruler over the glued ribbon and, with both palms, apply even pressure to help set the glue even better.

4. It is easy to pull up the ribbon and reglue if you have to as you work. Just be gentle!

5. If you do get glue on the fabric alongside the ribbon, simply blot it well with a damp cloth.

6. Proceed with this process until all the seams are covered with leading. Keep in mind that you will be covering the raw edges of short ribbons with the perpendicular longer ribbons adjacent to them.

7. You will need to reposition the quilt on the table as you work. Mondrian would be proud!

### Sew Down the Leading

Again, refer to Appliquéd Ribbon and Trim Leading on Pieced Blocks (page 33).

Up to this step you have been very careful to keep the quilt top as flat as possible and the leading straight and square. You can maintain that crispness while sewing if you keep in mind the following:

• Make sure the tension is right on your machine, so that the zigzag doesn't pull too tightly.

• Make sure the quilt travels easily under the needle by keeping it flat and unwrinkled. Try using binder clips to roll up and secure the side of the quilt top you have sewn, unrolling and reclipping as you progress across the quilt.

• Keep the fine-tip fabric glue bottle on hand by the machine to spot glue any ribbon that has pulled away from the fabric, leaving too large a gap. A tiny amount will do the trick.

• I use a quilting glove on my left hand as I sew. It helps me feed the fabric through the machine evenly on those long rows of zigzagging.

• Begin on the right-hand side of the quilt and sew down each side of the velvet ribbon in all the vertical rows. The ⅛″ ribbon requires only a single pass of zigzag set at 3 mm wide.

• Turn the quilt and sew down the horizontal ribbons.

# Quilt and Bind

Especially if you have used wiggly silk, the top will not be perfectly flat at this point. The quilting will even out the rumples and add some lovely texture.

1. Cut the backing fabric in half to make 2 pieces, 68″ long each.

2. Sew the 2 pieces together along the long edges to make the backing, and press the seam open.

3. Layer backing, batting, and quilt top, and pin baste.

4. Quilt as desired. I simply used channel quilting down the length of each rectangle.

5. Trim the quilt, and bind as desired. I used premade single-fold black binding.

6. Label your gorgeous quilt! Include your name, the date, and where it was made.

# A Variation to Consider

This table runner is essentially one large section. It was pieced and laid out on muslin as the complete quilt was, and finished exactly the same way. Although all the seams are leaded, the plaid is not leaded this time. It is a fun way to play with the concept of this project on a smaller scale.

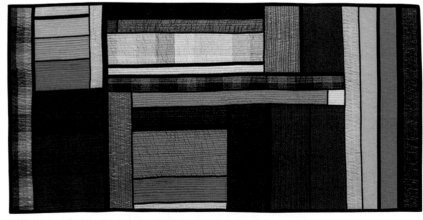

*Table Runner for Mondrian,* 22″ × 43½″, 2015

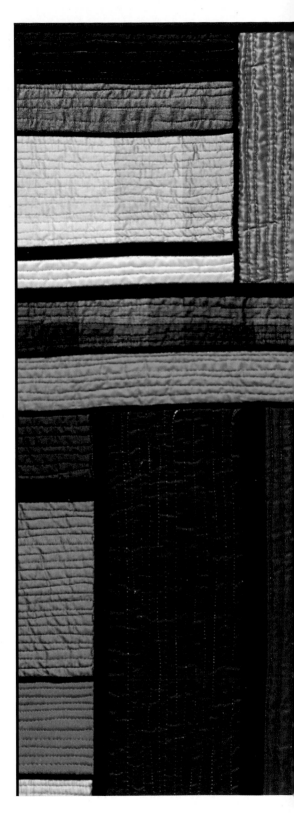

# Window for Frank

**Finished quilt:** 60˝ × 60˝

*Leading technique: Appliquéd ribbon (page 33)*

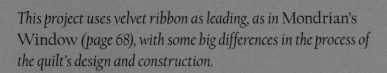

This project uses velvet ribbon as leading, as in Mondrian's Window (page 68), with some big differences in the process of the quilt's design and construction.

This is an improvisational quilt. You won't find a diagram or cutting instructions. Instead, I am presenting a formula for working that is logical yet spontaneous.

I have chosen to work in monochrome printed fabrics, all in cool tones, with my leading providing the color. Black velvet ribbon on the gray fabrics would look smashing as well. What color combinations are you drawn to?

Before you begin sewing, you will be cutting strips of fabric in various widths. After you sew some strips together, you will appliqué your ribbon leading of choice over those seams. So you will be appliquéing the ribbon as you go, not all at once on a finished quilt top. Review the technique for Appliquéd Ribbon and Trim Leading on Pieced Blocks (page 33).

You will cut pieced strip sets with their appliquéd ribbon into smaller units and then sew those together with other strips or units into a pattern. You will continue appliquéing ribbon leading over each set of new seams.

Because you will use consistent sizes and seam allowances for the strips (1½˝, 2½˝, and so forth, all with a ¼˝ seam allowance), the units will fit together well as they grow. There is no need for any foundation with this method, especially because nice sturdy cotton is used throughout the quilt, so there is no wiggly silk to contend with! If your units still aren't quite fitting together (mine didn't always), adding a plain strip where you need to fits right in with the overall design.

Your quilt top will evolve like a puzzle, in larger and larger sections as you sew the smaller ones together. You can add ribbon, as I have, to make triangles out of some of the pieced strips. Frank Lloyd Wright, whose distinctive stained glass window style inspired this quilt, often used this element.

## MATERIALS

*Yardage is based on 42˝-wide fabric, unless otherwise noted.*

**Assorted gray solid and print cotton fabrics:** at least 12, ranging in value from dark to very light, ¼ yard each

**Cool-colored velvet ribbons:** At least 12 in various widths, ⅛˝–1˝ wide, 7 yards each

**Backing:** 4 yards

**Low-loft batting:** 68˝ × 68˝

**Optional:** Binding, ½ yard

## Notions and Tools

**Fabric glue** (with a fine-tip applicator)

**Thread:**

• Clear thread for appliquéing ribbon and quilting

• 50-weight thread for piecing and bobbin

**Optional:** ¼˝ double-faced Sewing and Craft Tape (by Dritz) for long ribbons along binding

# Begin Making Units

*Seam allowances are ¼" unless otherwise noted.*

Here are instructions for two methods of piecing the units for this project.

## Pieced Units

1. Start by cutting a variety of strips in different widths out of the assorted gray fabrics: 1½" × 42", 3" × 42", 4" × 42", and 5" × 42" work well. Don't cut all the fabric yet, though!

2. Cut equal lengths from 3 of the strips, say 13". Sew the strips together to make a strip set. You can make your strip set longer or shorter. (This is improv piecing!) Trim the ends of the strip set even. Press the seams open.

3. Cut 2 pieces of velvet ribbon to length, a little longer than the seams in the strip set. Ribbons can be different widths and different colors.

4. Either glue baste or pin the ribbon into place over the seams.

5. Appliqué each edge of the ribbon with monofilament thread in a zigzag set at 1.5 (length) by 1.5 (width), or simply the narrowest width on your sewing machine. Press flat from the back of the fabric.

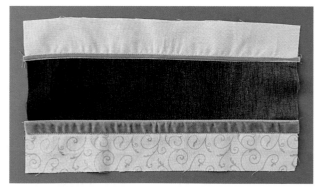

Strip set with leading

6. Cut the strip set into smaller, even units. You can have several skinny pieces or a couple of chunky pieces.

7. Take another random single strip that you cut in Step 1 and sew it in between the first 2 units. Cut off the extra length.

8. Sew the next length of the single strip to the second unit. Press the seams open from the back.

9. Add the third unit to the strip you have just sewn, and so on, alternating units and single strips.

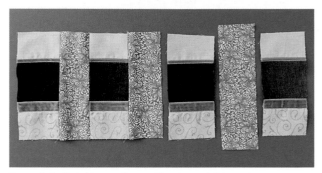

Steps 6–9: Combining the small units and the strips

10. When this new pieced unit is complete, go back and appliqué a variety of ribbons over all the new seams. Press flat from the back. Trim the ribbons even with the strip set.

Completed large unit

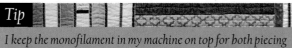

**Tip**

*I keep the monofilament in my machine on top for both piecing and appliquéing the ribbon. That way I don't have to constantly keep rethreading my machine.*

# Triangular Units

1. From the assorted gray fabrics, cut 2 strips of equal width × 42″ long. Cut equal lengths from the 2 strips, say 12″. Sew the strips together lengthwise. Press the seam open. *Note: The wider the strips, the larger the triangles will be.*

2. Draw a seam allowance ¼″ from the long outside edge of the strip set.

3. Starting ¼″ from the top of the strip set, center the corner of a square ruler over the seam so that you get a 45° triangle from each side of the ruler to the drawn line on the edge of the strip set. Mark all the way out to the drawn lines on the sides of the strip set.

4. Mark a horizontal line to connect the lines marked in Step 3, drawing the base of the triangle.

5. Measure ¼″ below the horizontal triangle baseline along the seam, and mark at dot. Center the corner of your ruler again at the dot.

6. Repeat Steps 3–5 all the way down the joined strips, drawing as many triangles on the strip set as will fit. Trim the bottom edge of the strip set ¼″ below the baseline of the last triangle.

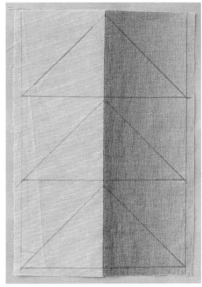

Steps 2–6: Triangles marked on pieced strips

---

## *Glue and Appliqué the Ribbon*

1. Cut a length of ribbon to cover one side of the first triangle. Miter the corner at the top and cut the side flush with the fabric.

2. Run a line of glue along the first diagonal line. Center a ribbon over the glue and finger-press into place. Use the edge of the ruler to keep the ribbons straight as you glue.

3. Repeat for the other side of the triangle. Don't worry about the raw edges of the mitered ribbons; they will be covered later.

4. Cut a length of ribbon to cover the base of the triangle, and glue it into place.

5. Repeat until all the triangles are covered.

Steps 1–5: Ribbons being glued over triangles

6. Appliqué the ribbons with monofilament thread using a narrow zigzag stitch.

7. Choose a different color and width of ribbon for the center seam. It will cover the raw edges of the ribbon at the tops of the triangles. (However, you could use the same color ribbon for this step on all the triangle units in your quilt, to add a unifying element.) Measure, cut, and glue into place.

8. Appliqué the center ribbon on each side.

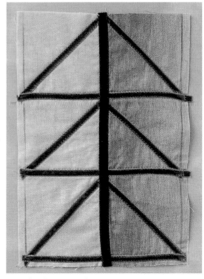

Finished triangular unit

# Assemble All the Prepared Units

When you have a small pile of pieced units, extra strips, and a few triangular units, it is time to fit them together like a puzzle. You may need to trim or add fabric here or there as you pin and sew.

Keep pressing as your quilt grows larger and larger. Always press from the back, or the ribbons will melt. Don't ever press from the front!

Use the floor or a design wall to rough out the placement of your units. You will discover for yourself how best to arrange them and what to add as you develop the rhythm of your quilt.

Continue until the top measures 60″ × 60″.

# Quilt, Bind, and Label

1. Cut the backing fabric in half lengthwise to make 2 pieces, each 2 yards long. Sew them together to make a piece that is 2 yards by about 80″, and press the seam. (I prefer to press that seam open, but that is a personal choice.)

2. Layer the backing, batting, and quilt top together. Pin baste.

3. Quilt and bind as desired. I used the same binding technique as in *Windy Sunshine* (see Bind and Label Your Quilt, page 58), trimming the backing, folding it to the front, and mitering the corners. Then I added trim to the edge of the binding on the front of the quilt.

> **Tip**
>
> *Instead of gluing my trim over the edge of the binding on the front of the quilt, I used Dritz Sewing and Craft Tape. This double-faced tape is very helpful for long lengths of ribbon. It is a simple matter to apply the thin double-sided tape along the edge of the binding and then press the velvet ribbon into place on top of it. The zigzag stitching on each side of the ribbon is a breeze: no pins needed, no shifting.*

4. Label your quilt, including your name, the date, and where the quilt was made.

Detail of the finished quilt, showing the quilting and a corner

# *Welcome Wreath*

**Finished wallhanging: 22¾″ × 22¾″**

*Leading technique: Iron-on leading (page 36)*

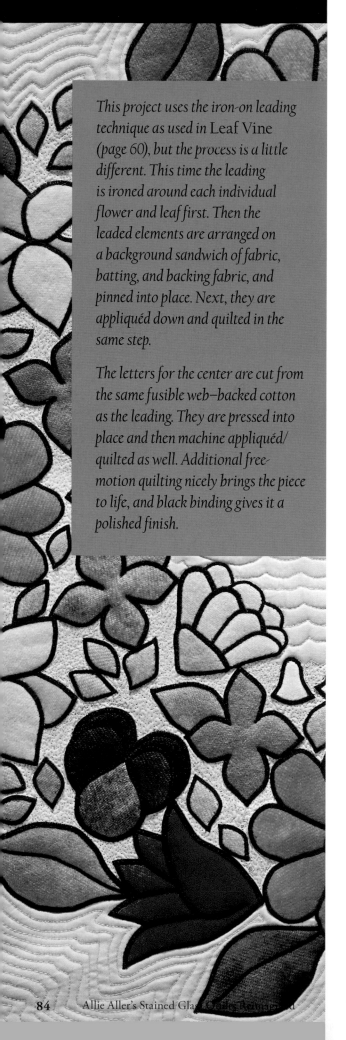

This project uses the iron-on leading technique as used in Leaf Vine (page 60), but the process is a little different. This time the leading is ironed around each individual flower and leaf first. Then the leaded elements are arranged on a background sandwich of fabric, batting, and backing fabric, and pinned into place. Next, they are appliquéd down and quilted in the same step.

The letters for the center are cut from the same fusible web–backed cotton as the leading. They are pressed into place and then machine appliquéd/quilted as well. Additional free-motion quilting nicely brings the piece to life, and black binding gives it a polished finish.

## MATERIALS

*Yardage is based on 42"-wide fabric, unless otherwise indicated.*

**Wool:** 18 pieces approximately 5" × 10" for flowers and leaves

**Black cotton:** 18" × 18" for lettering

**Fusible web:** 18" × 18"

**Sky-blue fabric:** 25" × 25" for background (I used Pretty Day from Shades Textiles. See Some of My Favorite Supplies, page 98.)

**Batting:** 25" × 25"

**Backing:** 25" × 25"

**Prepared binding:** Approximately 3 yards of your choice

### Notions and Tools

**Thread:**

- Smoke-colored monofilament thread for top

- Black 50-weight or finer for bobbin

- Clear monofilament thread for free-motion quilting

- Blue 50-weight or finer for bobbin

**Needle:** Size 60/8 or 70/10 universal needle

**Fabric marking pen**

**Chalk marker:** This is the easiest and best way that I've found to mark wool.

**Temporary fabric glue**

**Temporary spray fabric adhesive**

**Tracing paper, paper scissors, and pencil**

**Optional:**

- Freezer paper

- Mini-iron (recommended)

# Create the Stained Glass Flowers

## Make Your Templates and Leading

### Floral Motif Templates

Locate the floral motifs A1–K3 (pullout page P1).

1. Trace each leaf and flower onto tracing paper. Some flowers have 2 or 3 parts and are numbered. A1 and A2 go together, and E1 and E2 go together, for example. An arrow on the pattern indicates the orientation of the flower on the wreath. Trace the parts individually. Each flower and leaf pattern tells you how many pieces to cut out.

2. Cut out the templates. You don't need to add a seam allowance; just cut on the line.

3. *Optional:* If desired, glue the templates to the dull side of some freezer paper and cut them out again. This gives you the option of pressing the templates to the wool before cutting out the flowers. (You can easily lift them off and reuse them several times.) Otherwise, just pin the tracing paper to the wool and cut right around the template.

## Leading

You won't need a variety of leading widths for this project. I found that cutting my leading ⅛″ wide worked well. (See Making the Leading Strips, page 37.) A thinner leading for the center of the large leaves is the only exception.

1. Following the manufacturer's instructions, press the 18″ × 18″ fusible web to the back of the 18″ × 18″ black cotton.

2. Keep in mind that the *Welcome* lettering will also be cut from this piece of black fused fabric. Using a ruler, cutting mat, and rotary cutter, slice up a pile of leading ⅛″ wide. Imagine a hefty serving of black linguine—that's about how much you will need!

---

## Set Up Your Work Station

You will need an area to lay out the background/batting/backing sandwich, an ironing surface for creating the stained glass flowers, and a cutting mat nearby for cutting extra leading if you need it. Because the sewing comes last, you don't need your machine at this point.

---

## Make the Flowers

It's a good idea to try out this leading process by making a few sample flowers. When you are comfortable with the results, make the rest of them.

Some initial sample flowers

1. Pin templates A1 and A2 to the wool colors you have chosen.

Pinning the templates onto the wool

2. Cut them out and draw in the petal lines with chalk on A1.

3. Start the leading process with the circle A2. Cut the end of a piece of leading off at an angle. Working on your pressing surface, place the leading along the perimeter of the circle so that the leading barely hangs off the edge of the wool. Press the end into place.

4. Very gently pull the leading around the perimeter of the circle, keeping it flat and parallel to the surface of the wool. Follow along right behind with the iron. Don't tug on the leading! Just gradually bend it around the circle, pressing it into place as you go.

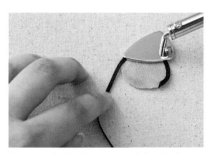

Pressing the leading around the circle

5. When you've gone all the way around the circle, overlap the beginning tip and clip the extra leading off at an angle, flush with the edge of the circle.

6. For the daisy, start pressing the leading on at the center, along a chalk line, and up around the first petal. Clip the end off at an angle into the V shape formed between this first petal and its neighbor.

7. For the second petal, again start in the daisy center and go up the next chalk mark and around the petal, covering the end of the first piece of leading in the V between the petals as you go. Clip at an angle in the next V.

8. Repeat Step 7, going all the way around the flower.

Steps 7 and 8: Applying leading to the petals marked with chalk

9. Put a small dot of the fabric glue on the back of the circle. Press the

leaded circle into place over the center of the daisy.

Completed daisy, ready for placement on background fabric

## Arrange and Appliqué the Flowers

### Prepare the Background

1. In the center of the sky-blue 25″ × 25″ piece, use a fabric pen to draw a 22½″ × 22½″ box. This gives you the margins for your wreath layout and will be the trimmed size of your wallhanging.

2. Find the exact center of the sky-blue 22½″ × 22½″ square and mark it with a dot. (I do this by folding the square into exact quarters and dotting the very tip of the folded corner in the center.)

3. Layer the sky-blue square (right side up), batting, and backing fabric (right side down). Pin baste the layers together around the outside of the box and put a pin by that center dot to anchor the center.

### Add the Flowers

Refer to the quilt photo as a guide for arranging the flowers, or create your own design.

1. Arrange the largest flowers first, measuring equidistant from the center dot and within the marked box. Use a few pins through all three layers to secure these big flowers.

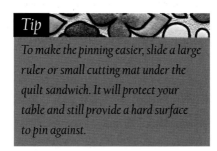

**Tip**

*To make the pinning easier, slide a large ruler or small cutting mat under the quilt sandwich. It will protect your table and still provide a hard surface to pin against.*

2. Arrange and pin the smaller flowers into place.

3. Continue until all the flowers and leaves are in place. You may find you need to make a few extra to fill in gaps here and there.

4. Before you begin to sew, I urge you to make a practice sample to make sure your stitch length and tension are good. You can also use the practice sample when you begin

the free-motion quilting, to make sure all is well. I set my sewing machine to a zigzag stitch about 2.5 wide and 1.5 long. The settings may be different on your machine. Use a fine machine needle with the smoke-colored clear thread on top, and black thread in the bobbin. Take it slowly, and sew down the leading around and within each flower and leaf.

Practice sample of appliquéd flower and free-motion quilting

**NOTE:** *The sewing is a little cumbersome at first with all those pins, but it gets easier as you get more and more flowers and leaves sewn down. Remember to remove the pins before you sew over them.*

# Create and Appliqué the Lettering

I love the idea of a welcome wreath hung on our door. But of course you can say anything you like inside your wreath.

## Cut Out the Letters

1. Use the *Welcome* pattern (pullout page P1). Trace the letters onto a piece of tracing paper.

2. Give the back of the paper with the traced letters a very light spritz of the temporary fabric adhesive spray. Smooth the paper over the right side of some of the fused black cotton fabric that you used for leading.

3. Cut out each letter and then gently pull off the tracing paper.

4. Use a ruler and a fabric marking pen to draw a line inside the wreath. Arrange the letters on the line.

5. Place a piece of tracing paper over the letters and gently press down with your iron. You don't want the letters to shift as you fuse them onto the background. The "pressing paper" helps avoid that.

6. Sew the letters down with a narrow zigzag using the smoke-colored invisible thread. I set my machine at 1.5 wide and 1.5 long. This is where having that fine machine needle is extra important.

> **Tip**
>
> *You can create your own letter templates by picking a suitable font you like on your computer in a program such as Microsoft Word. The font I used here was Princess Sofia in bold, at 134 points, with the W at 138 points. Simply print out your word or phrase in the font and sizes you like, and use those letters as your templates.*

# Quilt, Bind, and Label

1. Quilt within the drawn box of the layered piece. I used a simple microstipple in clear invisible thread between the flowers and leaves to make them pop out. I used echo quilting with a matching blue 50-weight cotton thread around the letters and outside the wreath.

2. Trim the quilted piece on the lines of the marked 22½″ × 22½″ box.

3. Bind as desired. I used premade black binding.

4. Label the quilt with your name, the date, and where the quilt was made.

# A Variation

I used gold leading in *Love Wreath* (page 47) for a softer version of the wreath, with the leading forming the letters *L-O-V-E* in the center of the wreath.

# Tiffany's Peacock

**Finished wallhanging:** 20˝ × 20˝

*Leading technique: Iron-on leading (page 36)*

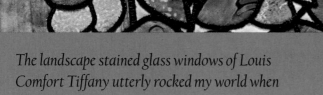

The landscape stained glass windows of Louis Comfort Tiffany utterly rocked my world when I first saw them in a book twenty years ago. As Tiffany said, "Color is to the eye as music is to the ear," and his colors have ravished me ever since.

Some of his favorite elements were peacocks, wisteria, and those receding planes in the background that always gave perspective. These translate into quilt design very nicely, especially when using the iron-on leading technique. We can easily vary the width of the leading: The background can be very thin, with the middle-ground leading thicker and the foreground the thickest of all. This all adds to the illusion of perspective and distance.

This quilt top is constructed in three layers. The background of sky, hills, trees, and wall are laid out first. The next layer, the middle ground, is comprised of the wisteria vines, leaves, and flowers. These are collaged onto the background with a glue stick. Iron-on leading is then applied to both layers and sewn down before the peacock is added to the composition.

Finally, in the foreground is the peacock. It is laid out on its own muslin foundation, exactly the way the background layer was: The main sections of fabric are spray basted into place, with the details added using a glue stick. Leading within the peacock is ironed on and sewn down. After the peacock has been trimmed to shape, it is glue basted into its place over the middle ground. Last, the leading is added and sewn around its perimeter.

Because this is the most advanced project in the book, I encourage you to review the information on transferring designs onto muslin (page 16), creating templates from your design (page 15), and the iron-on leading technique (page 36). Then set up your work space (page 52), take out the full-size pattern (pullout page P2), gather your colors, and let's make some music....

## MATERIALS

### Foundation muslin and iron-on leading

**Muslin:**

• 24″ × 24″ piece for foundation

• 16″ × 20″ piece for peacock

**Lightweight fusible interfacing:**

• 24″ × 24″ piece for foundation

• 16″ × 20″ piece for peacock

**Fusible web:** 16″ × 24″ piece for leading

**Solid black cotton:** 16″ × 24″ piece for leading

### Background

**Sky fabric:** 11″ × 20″

**Light/medium brown:** 6″ × 18″ for trees

**Light yellow/green:** From very pale to barely medium in value, 5 strips 3″ × 20″ for hills

**Light to medium gray:** 3 strips 4″ × 15″ for wall

### Middle ground

**Medium green/brown:** 9″ × 18″ for vine stems

**Medium blue/green:** 12–15 scraps 6″ × 8″ for leaves

**Pink and light to medium purple:** 8–10 scraps 10″ × 10″ for wisteria

### Peacock

**Dark blue, peacock blue, and blue green:** 6″ × 10″ each for body

**Orange/brown:** Small scraps for under wing

**Medium green / turquoise:** 10″ × 14″ for background of tail

**Medium and teal green:** 2″ × 8″ scraps for long tail feathers

**Royal blue (metallic lamé, optional), orange, and green:** 2″ × 8″ scraps for tail-feather eyes and crown

**White, black, aqua, and pale yellow:** 2″ × 3″ scraps for face

### Backing, batting, and binding

**Backing fabric:** 26″ × 26″ piece

**Thin cotton batting:** 26″ × 26″ piece

**Prepared binding:** Approximately 3 yards of your choice

## Notions and Tools

**Temporary fabric marking pen**

**Chalk marker** (or other marker that shows up on dark fabrics)

**Adhesives:** Temporary fabric adhesive spray, glue stick, long-tipped bottle of Roxanne Glue-Baste-It

**Tracing paper**

**Freezer paper**

**Lint roller** (for keeping work clean as you go)

**Needles:** 70/10 machine needles

**Thread:**

• Smoke-colored invisible thread

• Black lightweight thread for bobbin

**Optional:** Quilting glove

---

# The Background: Sky, Trees, Hills, and Wall

## Prepare the Muslin Foundation and Background Templates

1. Use the *Tiffany's Peacock* pattern (pullout page P2). Trace the lines of the background elements onto the 24″ × 24″ muslin with a disappearing fabric marker.

2. Following the manufacturer's instructions, fuse the 24″ × 24″ piece of lightweight fusible interfacing to the back of the muslin. This will make the sewing go smoothly and reduce any chance of distorting the foundation as you work on it.

3. Draw a 20″ × 20″ box in the center of the fabric side of the fused muslin square. Mark this square on the front and back of the muslin so the lines are super-imposed on each other. You'll be able to see the lines as you cover the front with collage pieces, but you'll be able to trim the square from the back in the final steps of the project. This line gives you the margins for the peacock composition and will be the trimmed size of your wallhanging.

4. In Transfer the Pattern Design to the Background Fabric (see the last option, page 16), we traced the entire shape of the turkey onto freezer paper to help guide the placement of the individual pieces within the turkey. This time, trace the outer shape of the peacock onto freezer paper and cut it out. You will lay this mock-up of the peacock over the muslin background so that you will know what will be covered by the foreground. This will save fabric when you are cutting out the hill shapes.

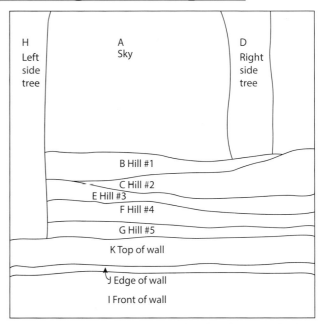

Diagram shows background pieces labeled in alphabetical order for assembly on muslin. This is how the pieces appear without the peacock. Note that the leading lines on the large sky piece are added later.

5. Referring to the Step 4 diagram and using the pattern (pullout page P2), trace the sky (A) onto tracing paper as a complete piece, going behind tree D. Add a ½″ seam allowance on the bottom edge and left side of A. This allows for subsequent pieces to overlap the sky A piece.

6. Using the peacock project pattern (pullout page P2), continue tracing hill pieces B, C, E, F, and G so that they go behind the foreground pieces, adding a ½″ seam

allowance at the bottom edge and the left side of each piece to allow subsequent pieces to overlap them. Trace the trees D and H, adding a ½″ seam allowance only on the bottom edges. The trees have no seam allowances on their long sides.

7. Trace wall pieces I and J so that they will tuck behind the position of the peacock, adding a ½″ seam allowance on the right and top edges of each piece. Trace wall piece K with only a ½″ seam allowance on the right edge.

8. Cut out each template piece and press the tracing-paper pieces flat.

---

## Cut Out and Spray Baste Background Fabrics

It is always best to work from the farthest-away to the closest elements in a landscape-style collage such as this. And what could be farther away than the sky?

1. Start by pinning the A template to the right side of the sky fabric and marking around it with the fabric marker. Pin and mark the B–K templates on the right side of the appropriate fabric pieces.

2. Cut out pieces A–K from the appropriate fabrics, referring to the quilt photo (page 88).

3. Spray the back of piece A with temporary fabric adhesive.

4. Smooth it in place on the marked foundation. Press it flat.

5. Continue adding pieces B–H in alphabetical order in like manner. Remember to overlap the top of the new piece over the bottom edge of the previous piece.

6. Place piece I in its position at the bottom of the marked foundation and secure in place.

7. Add piece J, overlapping the top edge of piece I. Finally, add piece K, overlapping pieces I and G on the foundation.

Background pieces glue basted onto muslin foundation

### Tip

*I prefer to use the temporary adhesive spray on larger shapes such as those in the background. They just stay flatter in place and I don't have to worry about wrinkling or shifting. But I don't like fusing because sometimes even those big shapes have to be moved or their edges lifted up while composing the collage. The glue stick is preferable for small shapes.*

*You can also very lightly spray the back of a tracing-paper template, smooth it onto the right side of the fabric, and simply cut out around it. Then peel off the template. This saves pinning and marking.*

# The Middle Ground:
# Vines, Leaves, and Wisteria Flowers

The vines provide the structure for the composition of the middle ground as well as for the vegetation. Therefore, it is important to make templates for them. Glue basting the backs of the fabrics will keep them in place.

The leaves and flowers are drawn out on the pattern, but if you feel confident using that as a visual reference, go ahead and cut yours out freehand and glue baste them to your collage. Keep the freezer-paper cut-out peacock shape nearby for reference as well, occasionally laying it in place to see how you are doing with your middle-ground layout.

## Lay Out the Middle Ground

### The Vines

1. Trace all the vines from the pull-out pattern onto tracing paper. No seam allowance is required.

2. Cut out the vine templates. Lay the vines on the right side of the vine fabric you wish to use and pin in place.

3. Carefully cut around the templates and remove the pins (or mark around the templates and then cut out the vines, if you prefer).

4. Lightly use a glue stick to glue the backs of the vines at short intervals, and then smooth them into place over the background, using the pullout pattern as a visual guide. Press flat.

### The Leaves and Wisteria

1. Whether you make leaf templates or cut them freehand, you need to cut out about 70 small leaves in various shades of green fabric, keeping them the same size and shape as shown on the pattern. Referring to the pattern, arrange them on the collage.

2. When they are in place and you are satisfied with their arrangement, dab the glue stick on the wrong side of the fabric leaves, a leaf at a time, and press them back into place.

3. The wisteria flowers are shaded from pink to light through dark purple, from the lower tip to the wide top of each raceme. You can trace the shapes and make little templates, as in the steps above, or you can refer to the pattern and cut them out freehand, and then use the pattern to guide placement. Once they are cut out and arranged, a shape at a time glue each little shape into place using the glue stick. Press in place.

4. When the entire middle-ground collage has been glued in place, press it flat by gently pressing and then lifting the iron—do not run the iron back and forth. The final preparation before the leading step is to lightly run a lint roller over the surface of the collage to pick up any threads.

Middle-ground collage glued in place over background, ready for leading

### Leading the Background and Middle Ground

This stage of the project uses the iron-on leading technique (page 36).

As in the previous stage, it is good to press the iron-on leading by starting with the background pieces and then moving to the middle-ground pieces. This is slow and repetitive work, but actually very relaxing. And it is fun to watch the design come into focus as the leading gets added.

1. Following the manufacturer's instructions, fuse the piece of

16″ × 24″ fusible web to the reverse side of the 16″ × 24″ black cotton.

2. Using a rotary cutter and mat, cut several leading strips 1/16″ wide from the fused black fabric.

3. Press these 1/16″ leading strips along the "seams" between all the background pieces on the pieced foundation.

4. Add a few extra-fine lines of 1/16″ leading to the large sky section (see the quilt photo, page 88, for a visual reference.)

5. Cut a large pile of leading strips 1/8″ wide from the fused black fabric.

6. Refer to Now You Try It, Step 6 (page 40) to see how to get those sharp points and tight curves with the leading. Then press 1/8″ leading

strips on all the elements of the middle ground, leaves, the wisteria flowers, and the wall, from the bottom of the composition to the top.

7. Gently press your work flat with a gentle up-and-down motion of the iron.

8. Set this foundation section aside for now while the peacock is constructed.

# The Peacock

## Overview of the Process

The reason the peacock is worked on a separate foundation is its intricate detail. Applying the leading and then zigzag stitching around those concentric teardrop shapes on the tail is so much easier on a smaller piece of work.

After the interior is leaded and the leading is sewn down, the peacock is spray basted into place on the larger work. The beak, face, and crown are then added, and the entire peacock is leaded around its perimeter. After one final pressing, the last of the leading will be sewn down.

### Prepare the Foundation, Templates, and Main Fabric Shapes

1. Trace the 5 main peacock sections from the pattern (pullout page P2) onto the 16″ × 20″ piece of foundation muslin, using the temporary fabric marking pen.

2. Following the manufacturer's instructions, fuse the piece of 16″ × 20″ lightweight fusible interfacing to the back of the marked muslin.

3. Trace the 5 main peacock sections onto tracing paper to make templates. Add a 1/4″ seam allowance where a section is overlapped by another. Cut out the sections using paper scissors.

4. Very lightly spray baste or pin each template to your fabrics of choice for each section, and cut out.

5. Spray baste and place the fabric sections onto the foundation in numerical order.

6. Use a chalk or temporary fabric marker to draw the little "scale" lines (they are really tiny feathers, but they look like scales) on Sections 1, 4, and 5, referring

to the pullout pattern and the diagram below.

7. Press the pieces flat.

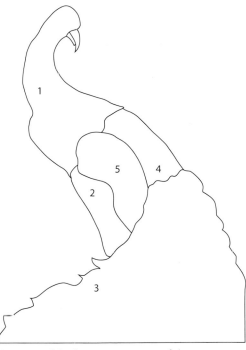

Diagram of the five main sections of the peacock, showing the order of placement on the foundation

## THE FEATHERS

Now that the main sections of the peacock are in place on the muslin foundation, you will be cutting feathers to give greater detail to Sections 2 and 3 of the peacock (see diagram, page 93). Refer to the quilt photo (page 88).

1. As before, either trace the feather shapes from the pullout pattern for the individual wing feathers of Section 2 and tail feathers of Section 3, *or* use the pullout pattern as a visual reference to freehand cut your own. The "eyes" of the feathers will come in the last step, so wait on those yet.

2. Cut and arrange the orange feathers for the Section 2 wing area. You may find yourself trying out a few different fabrics before you settle on the ones you want to use.

3. Arrange the tail feather shapes onto Section 3, the tail. Again, you may find yourself trying out a few different fabrics before you settle on the ones you want to use. (I went through 3 sets of different colors before I got the look I wanted.) Play with the feather shapes until your arrangement is just right. Press it flat.

4. Rather than lifting the entire feather arrangement, use the long tip of the Glue-Baste-It bottle to gently lift the feathers individually, while they are still in place, and dot some glue to the background fabric behind them.

5. Press flat. This helps set the glue, too.

Peacock with feathers on separate foundation

6. It's time to add leading to the peacock interior, but *you will not add leading to the outside edges of the peacock.* Add the ⅛" leading on the feather shapes as you did with the middle-ground shapes.

7. Add very thin ¹⁄₁₆" leading over the marked "scales" on Sections 1, 4, and 5.

8. Use ⅛" leading to outline Sections 4 and 5.

### Create the Eyes of the Tail Feathers

Each "eye" is made of three concentric teardrop shapes. Because they are so small, it is easier to fuse these tiny shapes into place before leading, rather than try to glue them.

1. Refer to the quilt photo (page 88) for color reference. Select and prepare your 3 eye fabrics by fusing the fusible web to the reverse side of each fabric, following the manufacturer's instructions.

2. Refer to the pattern (pullout page P2) to locate 3 patterns for the tail feather eyes. On most of the eyes, the longest teardrop (blue) is 1½" long, the middle teardrop (orange) is ¾", and the smallest teardrop (green) is ½". But notice that these eyes all become slightly smaller toward the body. The largest eyes are at the bottom edge of the composition, so you need to slightly vary the sizes of the eyes on the tail. There are 3 sizes of eye patterns on the pullout page, but you can make templates or not. Cut 35 teardrops of each size.

3. Arrange the blue teardrops over the entire tail section, on top of the layer of feathers. When you have the arrangement you like, fuse them down.

4. Fuse an orange teardrop on top of a blue one, leaving ⅛" of blue showing at the base. Repeat for the rest of the orange teardrops.

5. Fuse the green teardrops into place on top of the orange ones, with their bases touching.

### Apply the Leading to the Eyes

1. Cut the thinnest leading strips you can, about ¹⁄₁₆".

2. Very slowly, press the leading around the green teardrops within each eye. Picking up the peacock

and turning it halfway through is easier than trying to iron down the teardrop all at once.

3. If your leading should pull apart (it is quite fragile when it is this thin), simply iron a new piece overlapping where the first leading came apart, and keep going.

Detail of a section of the completed tail

**Add Extra Lines to the Tail**

When the tail is all leaded, study it to see how you can add more complexity and movement to it. Doing this is easy: Cut the thinnest leading strips you can, and iron on more lines within the feather shapes. You may wish to add more lines to the wing feathers too.

THE PEACOCK FACE, BEAK, AND CROWN

1. Refer to the peacock pattern (pullout page P2). Using tracing paper, trace the shapes for the face first. Before cutting the eye into smaller pieces, use the entire shape as a template on white fabric to cut a base for the eye construction. Then cut the smaller fabric pieces of aqua blue, orange, and black for the mask, eye, and eyeball, and glue baste them onto the white foundation.

2. Lay the face onto the peacock head to see how it looks. If you don't like it, make another one, changing what you didn't like. (It took me 6 tries.) When you are happy with it, glue baste the pieced foundation into place on the peacock.

3. Add the thin leading around the shapes of the face and eye.

4. Trace the shapes for the beak and the crown onto tracing paper and cut the templates out. Use the templates to cut the pieces from the appropriate fabrics. Set these pieces aside; they will be added after the peacock is in place on its background.

# Sew It All Down

## Sew the Peacock

You will sew the leading on the interior of the peacock while it is still separate from the foundation. Use the smoke-colored invisible thread for the top thread and the lightweight black thread in the bobbin. Zigzagging all these details is not quick, but it is very straightforward. At this point, there is no leading on the outside edges of the peacock. Refer to Sew Down the Leading (page 42).

The interfacing helps to keep the peacock flat as you sew down the leading. Wearing a quilting glove on one hand makes turning the work much easier as you zigzag around the intricate curvy shapes. There is a lot of starting and stopping as you sew. Clip the top and bobbin threads as you go to keep your work neat. Press the peacock unit flat from the muslin side.

## Sew the Background and Middle Ground

Sew the leading on the background and middle ground before you layer the peacock over them. Again, take your time, go slowly, and listen to some nice music as you work. How about some Debussy music? I'll bet Tiffany liked it....

## Add Final Details and Sew the Peacock into Place

1. From the back of the large muslin pieced foundation, trim on the marked lines for the 20″ × 20″ square.

2. On the peacock unit, trim away the extra muslin foundation until you have the final shape of the peacock.

3. Position the peacock on the pieced foundation. Make sure the peacock is positioned just right. You may need to trim the bottom edge and right side edge of the peacock to be even with the muslin square.

4. Run the glue stick over the back of the peacock's foundation in several places. Position the peacock in its place and gently smooth it down with your hands.

5. Add the beak and the crown to the peacock's head with the glue stick, and iron on ⅛″ leading to complete the head.

Detail of the peacock head with face, beak, and crown in place and leaded (shown actual size)

6. Finally, cut several ⅛″ to ¼″ strips of leading and iron them around the perimeter of the peacock. Notice that the leading is slightly thinner at the top, so as not to dominate the head.

7. Zigzag stitch around the perimeter leading of the peacock.

# Finishing

## Quilt, Bind, and Label

> **NOTE:** *Because I wanted my peacock quilt to stay extra flat, I fused a second layer of interfacing to the back of the completed top. This ensured that my wallhanging would hang very straight and that there would be minimal wrinkles or puckering as I quilted. You might want to try it.*

1. Layer the top, batting, and backing together. Spray basting the layers together works well, but you may pin baste them if you prefer.

2. The quilting is quick because it only surrounds the main shapes within the picture. There is no quilting within the peacock at all. Its three layers of interfacing keep it from sagging and even give it a slight dimensionality. Use a clear invisible thread on top and thread that matches the backing fabric in the bobbin. Quilt along the outside leading edges of the wisteria, vines, clumps of leaves, trees, hills, and sky sections, and around the peacock itself.

3. In keeping with the traditional nature of this project, I have given it the standard traditional black bias binding with mitered corners. You may bind as desired.

4. Label the quilt with your name, the date, and where the quilt was made.

*The End*, 20½″ × 23½″, 2016

## Conclusion

The more you work and play with these new techniques for stained glass quilting, the more new discoveries will unfold for you. I hope you will expand on what you've seen and read in these pages!

Here is one more idea to conclude this book: Iron-on leading can be treated as pure line on a wholecloth background, with no glass fabric appliquéd at all. In essence, you can create your own quilt coloring book page, as I have done here. The iron-on leading functioned as a great resist, so that as I painted in my colors, the thickened craft ink didn't spread "outside the lines."

Thank you so much for joining me here!

—Allie

The inspiration came from the book *Paisleys and Other Textile Designs from India* by K. Pradesh (Dover Publications, 1994). I used Tsukineko ink thickened with clear aloe vera gel from the drugstore and a very small paintbrush for coloring in my design.

# A Few of My Favorite Supplies

*I was fortunate to use wonderful products in the making of this book. Here is where you can find many of them.*

**AURIFIL**   *aurifil.com*

I used Monofilament Invisible Thread, my favorite brand, throughout this book.

**CLOVER**   *clover-usa.com*

Both the Wedge iron and the Mini Iron are great tools for iron-on leading.

**HANDI QUILTER**   *handiquilter.com*

I used the Sweet Sixteen sit-down mid-arm to quilt all my projects.

**KREINIK**   *kreinik.com*

The #16 braid and ⅛″ and ¼″ metallic ribbon are perfect for couching and appliquéing when you want some sparkle in your leading. See *Man of My Dreams* (page 3) and *Sunrise for Frances* (page 48).

**M&S SCHMALBERG**   *customfabricflowers.com*

Custom fabric flowers. Be sure to check out the Petals and Leaves gallery on the website. You can order any shape in your own fabric, too. I used some of the company's flower shapes in *Modern Rose Window* (page 44), with their kind permission.

**MICHAEL MILLER FABRICS**

*michaelmillerfabrics.com*

The Cotton Couture collection gave me clear and beautiful solid colors for *Henri's Window* (page 9) and *Modern Rose Window* (page 44).

**ROBERT KAUFMAN FABRICS**

*robertkaufman.com*

The silk/cotton blend called Radiance is an irreplaceable element in many of the projects in this book, especially as glass in *Mondrian's Window* (page 68) and as the background for *Modern Rose Window* (page 44) and *The End* (page 97).

**SHADES TEXTILES**   *shadestextiles.co*

Shades Textiles makes Soft Fuse, the paper-backed fusible web I use for all the iron-on leading. The company also makes a beautiful hand-dyed sky fabric called Pretty Day, which I used as the background foundation fabric in *Easter Sunrise* (page 46), *Fern Vine* (page 67), *Welcome Wreath* (page 83), and *Tiffany's Peacock* (page 88). You can also find it pieced into *Windy Sunshine* (page 53).

**WONDERFIL SPECIALTY THREADS**

*wonderfil.ca*

Wonderfil's fine Invisafil 100% polyester thread is my bobbin thread of choice, and the company's 50-weight cotton is my favorite for quilting and piecing.

**THE ANTIQUE PATTERN LIBRARY**

*antiquepatternlibrary.org*

This nonprofit website scans and preserves craft patterns that are in the public domain, thus preserving our craft heritage for free personal use. The organization has kindly allowed the publication of a design from *Dessins de Vitrerie* by Henri Carot used in *Henri's Window* (page 9).

Detail of *Henri's Window*

# About the Author

Photo by Robert Aller

ALSO BY ALLIE ALLER:

Ever since she was a design student in college, **Allie Aller** has been exploring many genres in quiltmaking. She is the author of *Allie Aller's Crazy Quilting* and coauthor with Valerie Bothell of *Quilting ... Just a Little Bit Crazy*, both from C&T Publishing, and teaches crazy quilting for Craftsy. She lives at the mouth of the beautiful Columbia River Gorge with her husband, Robert. Visit her blog at alliesinstitches.blogspot.com.

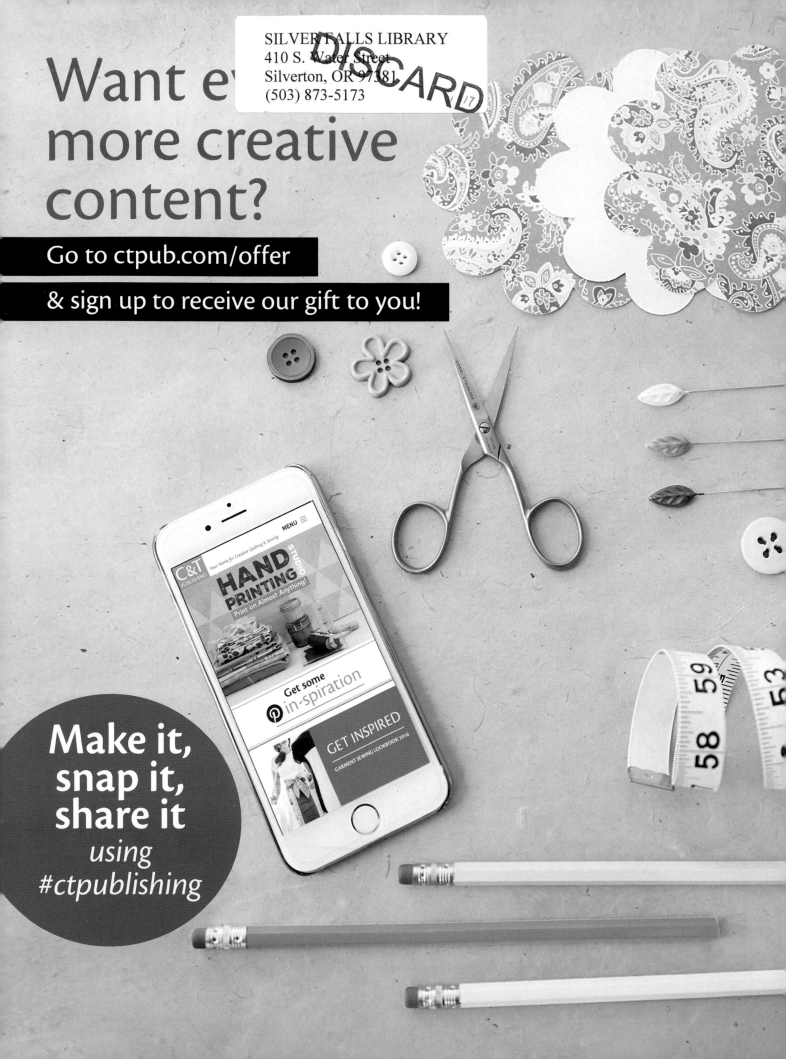

# Want ev... more creative content?

## Go to ctpub.com/offer

## & sign up to receive our gift to you!

## Make it, snap it, share it
*using*
*#ctpublishing*